EMIL BAGIROV

HANDBOOK
FOR PRACTITIONERS OF
CLASSIC COSMOENERGY
BY SCHOOL OF EMIL BAGIROV

VOLUME I

COMPILED BY

TETYANA ZINCHENKO AND MARIA ASADOV

LIBRARY OF INTERNATIONAL CLASSIC COSMOENERGY FEDERATION

EMIL BAGIROV

HANDBOOK
FOR PRACTITIONERS OF CLASSIC COSMOENERGY
BY SCHOOL OF EMIL BAGIROV

VOLUME I

Compiled by:
Tetyana Zinchenko and Maria Asadov

Translated by:
Maria Asadov and Oksana Zhukovych

Book Cover Design: Boris Andreev, © 2014, Toronto, ON

The book describes the methodology of Classic Cosmoenergy as defined by the Classic Cosmoenergy School by Emil Bagirov. It includes theory as well as practical rules and recommendations for working with the informational component of the Universe, the so-called "channels." The handbook is intended for all students of Classic Cosmoenergy School by Emil Bagirov.

INTERNATIONAL CLASSIC COSMOENERGY FEDERATION:

Secretary in USA: Alan Hunzicker
Russia, Moscow
Tel (Fax) 7 (495) 624 84 21,
Tel 7 (499) 121 12 13; 7 (495) 326 21 90 www.bagirovemil.ru e-mail: bagem@yandex.ru
Latvia, Riga: +371 26100461; +371 20011132
www.iccfworld.com
© Emaĭ l Bagirov, 2014
Copyright © 2014 by Emil Bagirov
Library of Congress Control Number: 514092261
ISBN: Softcover 978-1-63315-400-1

This book was printed in the United States of America.
To order additional copies of this book, contact:
Anders Printing Company, LLC
3402 SE Division Street
Portland, OR 97202
www.andersprinting.com

Table of Contents

FORWARD FROM COMPILERS

Dear Students of the Classic Cosmoenergy School by Emil Bagirov!

You are about to begin your journey to learn about Classic Cosmoenergy, a unique method, which activates a person's inner potential, relieves tension and stress, and transforms pathological processes leading to diseases and problems. This method has been proved to remove depression, bad mood, anxieties, and phobias and to help a person solve their various life problems.

The effectiveness of Classic Cosmoenergy has been confirmed by time, numerous patients' testimonials, and various scientific studies conducted by the International Classic Cosmoenergy Federation. Numerous scientific studies and eight patents that have been received (two in Russian Federation and six in European Union) prove not only the reality and objectivity of channels, but also their effect on restoring one's health. In 2009 the International Classic Cosmoenergy Federation has been officially admitted to the highest medical institution - World Health Organization (WHO). Now the International Classic Cosmoenergy Federation is an official member of the World Health Organization. Please note that he description of all scientific studies and patents conducted by Emil Bagirov are not included in this book, however, they are available on the website of the International Classic Cosmoenergy Federation (www.iccfworld.com).

As you might already know the method of Classic Cosmoenergy is not associated with any religions or saints and is accessible to everyone who wishes to learn it. The names of all channels used in the method are only arbitrary. In addition, it does not deny nor replace modern medicine and it is not used to diagnose, prescribe, cancel or change the dosage of any medications that were prescribed to the patient by their attending doctor.

This handbook is intended for the students of the Classic Cosmoenergy School by Emil Bagirov, i.e. for everyone who has been initiated by the Teachers of this school. The use of techniques described here without receiving initiations from a living Teacher in the direct chain of succession is fraught with severe consequences. We would like to remind you that receiving initiations from a living Teacher implies direct contact with a Teacher in person, not via Internet or phone. All training and initiations into this method should be received only from one Teacher. Receiving initiations from numerous different teachers obstructs the effectiveness of the method described in the book.

When using the handbook, it is important to follow all the rules without any modifications or additions. In addition, all beginners working with this method are required to consult with their Teacher for obtaining answers to any, even seemingly silly, questions, which arise during their studies and practical usage of the method.

We wish you success on your path to knowledge!

Tetyana Zinchenko and Maria Asadov

CLASSIC COSMOENERGY

In his time, Confucius formulated his Golden Rule in the "Talks and opinions": " One should treat others as one would like others to treat oneself". This is an ideal rule for an individual, combining both spiritual and moral greatness providing the right for higher social status.

Cosmoenergy is a method based on the use of so-called cosmic "energy-informational" fields or "channels" that possess healing properties. The healing processes are realized with help of yet-to-be-determined by science but quite material physical mechanisms of interaction "Cosmoenergy practitioner – patient." The most probable hypothesis suggests that such interactions use "something" from the arsenal of the already recognized but scientifically untested by physical information-enthalpy fields called "channels." It would probably be appropriate to expect a real manifestation of material traces of "dark cosmic matter" in this case.

According to current scientific studies, the matter visible to us is only one part of that which makes up our world. The remaining part is something that we know almost nothing about. This mysterious "something" was named "dark matter."

Looking back in the history, we will note that the greatest scientific discoveries were the result of the most insignificant controversies. As such, in 16th century, Copernicus suggested that Earth was not located in the center of the Universe, a model based on the measured movement of celestial bodies. Dr. Niels Bohr's, the physicist, developed ideas about the notion of complementarity that were considered "wild and fantastical" and dismissed as: "If the absurd that Bohr has just published is correct, then we can quit our careers as physicists right now, <...> throw all physics into a landfill and go there ourselves" (Otto Stern, 1913 Nobel prize laureate). The theory of thermodynamics was followed by statements like "Nonsense under the guise of science" (F.I. Fedorov, B.I. Stepanov, Academy of Sciences Magazine, Belorussian Soviet Socialistic Republic, 1974, #5, p. 131-133).

At the end of the 20th century – beginning of the 21st century, yet another revolution commenced with the discovery that the expansion of the Universe was accelerating. As a result of observing small variations in the brightness of the exploding stars, astronomers developed a theory demonstrating that 74% of the energy in our Universe is unknown. All space is filled with some "substance", exotic "energy" which varies from all substance known to science and generates a repulsion effect. This substance was named "dark energy" by science.

In 2011 American scientists Saul Perlmutter from University of California in Berkley and Adam Raines from Johns Hopkins University in Baltimore together with Brian Schmidt from Australian National University became the Nobel Prize laureates in physics for proving the accelerated expansion of the Universe.

According to data from the NASA spacecraft WMAP (Wilkinson Microware Anisotropy Probe) designated to study the relict radiation formed as a result of the Big Bang, the Universe consists of 74% of dark energy, 22% of dark matter, 3.6% of intergalactic gas, and only 0.4% of stars, planets, comets, etc. Fourteen years have passed since the discovery of dark energy, but science still does not exactly know what dark energy is.

Success of the therapeutic method of Cosmoenergy was confirmed by many scientific studies that were first conducted by the Classic Cosmoenergy School by Emil Bagirov and Institute of Psychology and Cosmoenergy and later continued by the International Classic Cosmoenergy Federation. Cosmoenergy today has a solid evidence base for confirming the existence of cosmic energy channels. The widespread and real success of Cosmoenergy treatment sessions for health improvement purposes has been recorded in thousands of documents from various Cosmoenergy centers of the Classic Cosmoenergy School by Emil Bagirov in Russia and abroad.

Eight patents have been received – two in Russian Federation and six in European Union – that prove not only reality and objectivity of channels, but also their restorative effects on a patient's health. The study "Dynamics of psycho-physiological rates of patients with neurotic disorders under impact of Cosmoenergy treatment sessions" was published in various scientific journals, including the journal "Medical Sciences" in section "Psychiatry." This study showed the effectiveness of neurotic disorders and depression treatment. To prove effectiveness of neurotic disorders treatment with help of Cosmoenergy treatment sessions, three hundred patients were treated using the Cosmoenergy treatment sessions over three years.

The study "Possibilities of Cosmoenergy treatment sessions in restoring person's health" published in the journal "Medical Science" (2011, #6) also demonstrates the method's restorative effects. Later, the scientific studies of this method resulted in several patents – patent of the Russian Federation #2270804 from 27 February, 2006 "Method for obtaining activated liquid" and patent received in European Union #CIG 01N 33/50 from February 15, 2007 "Method for determining effectiveness of the chronic gastritis and reflex esophagitis treatment" and others.

Since 2001 the International Classic Cosmoenergy Federation has been conducting clinical research in various medical institutions in Russia and other countries. More than ten years of scientific studies of several thousand patients have provided considerable statistical data. The results of these studies are periodically published in a number of Russian journals, such as "Medical Sciences", "Actual Problems of Modern Science", "Natural and Exact Sciences", "Graduate Student and Applicant", etc. Many scientific studies have been published on websites such as www.bagirovmil.ru and www.iccfworld.com. Based on the materials of scientific studies, monographs "Cosmoenergy phenomena" in two volumes have been published. Scientific studies of the method's results continue to this day. The results of the studies prove again and again the objectivity and effectiveness of the Classic Cosmoenergy method.

In 2009 the International Classic Cosmoenergy Federation has been officially recognized and admitted to the highest medical institution – World Health Organization (WHO). Now the International Classic Cosmoenergy Federation is an official member of the World Health Organization.

Attention! The use of channels without receiving Initiations and training from a skilled Teacher in the direct chain of succession can result in negative unintended consequences.

ABOUT THE COSMOENERGY METHOD

Today's medicine is at a very important stage in its treating methods progression. But traditional medicine is still, unfortunately, based on the old, Newtonian scientific paradigm. Inevitably, the new epoch has put forth demands for its expansion, at the very least. Today, we need to develop treatment methods based on the new principles of a new scientific paradigm, which is emerging in our day and age.

Once, people thought Einstein was crazy – so radical did his theory seem to be. Today, people view Cosmoenergy in approximately the same way. This happens when a scientific theory comes ahead of its time – physicists had needed almost 60 years to reason out Einstein's discoveries in a calm, cool-headed manner. Today, everyone claims to "understand" Einstein, and considers him a genius.

Cosmoenergy, in its own way, is ahead of its time, which explains why the path of its development was not strewn with roses. Unfortunately, the process of a person's development is not always pain-free. This is true not only for individuals but for cultures at large. According to a new scientific paradigm, energy and information (i.e. program formations) are seamlessly integrated and a person's physiology incorporates a complex system of informational energy fields, including genes (program formations). Thankfully, the more supporters this new scientific paradigm has, the more people, including medical doctors, there are who decline the use of medication and surgical procedures with dangerous side-effects in favor of more subtle methods of healing that are closer to nature. Cosmoenergy allows us to not only ease physical ailments, but to define and eliminate the root causes of illnesses, which lie hidden in the emotional, mental or other subtle planes.

Specialists in the sphere of Cosmoenergy are not just physicians, they are healers; they are able to combat not only physical ailments, but emotional and mental disorders as well. The latter will sooner or later manifest themselves on the physical plane as a disease of some sorts. The Cosmoenergy specialist is able to determine the causes for the illness and explain to their patients what changes need to be made to their lifestyle in order to reestablish harmony; how to eat better, which form of physical exercises would be the most beneficial, how to control one's emotions, how to de-stress oneself, and how to meditate in order to remove the true roots of their distress and suffering.

Cosmoenergy specialists search for the reasons of the disruption of harmony in the body by analyzing the state of the patient's chakras (controlling centers). However, despite the inarguable achievements Cosmoenergy has made in the realm of healing, we should never forget the *most important condition for a successful recovery – is the mandatory readiness of the patient to take full responsibility for their actions and lifestyle, which often lie at the source of their illnesses.*

Patients must be willing to work alongside the Cosmoenergy specialist healing them in order to re- introduce the lost state of harmony to their body and soul. But that is still not enough. One must rely on the teachings concerning reincarnation, according to which the soul makes a long journey of deaths and rebirths before it finally accumulates the necessary experience, as many illnesses stem from past lives during the process of reincarnation. *Only with that understanding, and with the realization of the true meaning of the soul's difficult path through a succession of bodies, can we find the internal strength to change our behavior and to find harmony again.*

The woes and troubles of our uneasy times are in many ways determined by the spiritual and emotional distress of the population. But, thankfully, people have the chance to be cured of such illnesses by means of receiving certain knowledge. For this to happen, it is very important to understand and eliminate the root causes of the illnesses, which lie not only on the surface physical level, but which also lie hidden on more subtle levels. Prior to becoming a true Cosmoenergy specialist – a practicing healer, a person must first go through an inner, spiritual change. Many Cosmoenergy specialists are already feeling the beginnings of such transformation; they have become adherents of a certain way of thinking and work to help individual people as well as humanity as a whole in their transition to a state of peace and harmony. Such self-actualization of Cosmoenergy specialists serves the good cause of maintaining our little planet's worthy existence.

Cosmoenergy as a science can help people find answers to the eternal questions of life and death. When used correctly, Cosmoenergy methods can return many people to health and spiritual peace, which would be hefty contribution to the well being of humanity on the entire planet for many centuries to come. Knowledge of Cosmoenergy channels has been around since ancient times, but was long kept in deep secrecy by a handful of "chosen people". The time now comes when this information should be in demand. But it is necessary that humanity understand the nature of the responsibility it takes upon itself with the use of this information, now, on the brink of a New Era, by resurrecting ancient methods of healing which had been given to it by the Great Masters of the Universe.

Most often, people turn to a healer to be rid of their suffering. In doing so, they forget that they should start with changing the way they think and the way they live. The success of the cure is greatly dependent on the nature of the collaboration between healer and patient, on their interaction. People should heed and follow their healer's advice, but *the responsibility for their way of life lies only on themselves.* Our illnesses are often the surface manifestations of deep spiritual or mental disorders, stresses or anxieties. As a general rule, the manifestation of an illness is caused by some sort of external factor, the effect of which will become truly serious only in the case that it lands in "fertile soil" within the person themselves.

Emotional problems and spiritual anxieties move through the system of chakras into the physical plane, where they cause a disruption to homeostatic balance called an illness. The vast majority of illnesses are the result of a malfunction in the work of the chakras, which control a multi-dimensional complex of the physical body plus the informational energy body plus the soul. What we perceive as an illness is a sort of warning light to the person, indicating that something is off in their multi-dimensional complex (the physical and informational energy bodies and the soul), and that the disrupted homeostasis ought to be set right, otherwise they will not be fully cured.

Many emotional and spiritual problems that people have are connected with the malfunction of chakras. Most of the time, these problems stem from the grossness and earthliness of people's consciences, sexuality, love, willpower, creativity, intuition and spiritual seeking; when a person finds themselves incapable of free self-expression in any of these areas, they become irritated. This, in turn, leads them to having more negative thoughts and emotions more often than usual, which allows for serious negative formations in their aura. The negative formations can and usually do go on to create a negative impact on the physical body, for example – developing into an illness.

We should also keep in mind that often-serious afflictions could be a form of spiritual trials, which the soul has to overcome in the process of its reincarnation. The heart chakra is a person's most important chakra, as it accumulates the experiences of our past lives. Yogis call the heart chakra – the chakra of knowledge; it determines the level of a person's spiritual development, which, in turn, determines the person's ability to love and express their love towards both those close to him as well as towards strangers. The state of this chakra determines a person's capacity for spiritual growth and enlightenment.

A poorly developed heart chakra often invokes fear in a person. Fear and a lack of desire to understand another person are the main sources of many illnesses, stresses and human suffering. People on the lower rungs of their spiritual development have a tendency to project their fears on the outside world, refusing to see that the causes of their sufferings lie only in themselves.

The development of the fourth chakra is the best way of clearing away such fears. The first thing it requires is the introduction of love and compassion into the person's life. By developing our heart chakras, we attain the ability to heal not only ourselves, but also others around us.

Evil deeds and bad behavior towards other people can manifest themselves in our future lives as congenital illnesses and deficiencies – this is a sort of karmic lesson. As a reward for honorable conduct in a past life, a person will be given the opportunity to attain wealth and success. Reincarnation teachings allow people to understand that their current suffering is a part of their spiritual trials, which every soul must go through and overcome. But a person can choose how they should act in every given situation: whether to use it towards the enrichment of their spiritual experience or not.

Many ancient civilizations such as the peoples of Atlantis, Lemuria, and the members of the secret sects of Egypt and Greece knew of reincarnation and of the multi-dimensional human anatomy. Despite all of humanity's sins, despite the many wars fought and the violence we experience, the "enlightened", those who know of man's divine nature and of the inexhaustibility of our spiritual potential, have always been active among the peoples of our world.

There is no doubt that Cosmoenergy takes its roots from Tibet and India, which are traditionally considered the proverbial "gates" to other worlds and civilizations. About four hundred years ago, what we call Cosmoenergy channels were first given to yogis by representatives of an extraterrestrial civilization, which the yogis and the locals of Tibet and India have named *Shambala*.

Rumors that there are people in India and Tibet that have very unusual methods of creating what we would call miracles and which cannot be explained by science have spread far beyond the borders of India and Tibet themselves. Which is why it is no coincidence that there has been a great interest shown towards these two countries for several centuries, first and foremost by England. Later, in the nineteenth and twentieth century Germany and Russia also took a great interest in Tibet and India.

After the Russian revolution, the young Soviet State Republic created a laboratory that was called "Laboratory for the Study of Ancient Knowledge", headed by professor Alexander Vasilievich Barchenko. The goals set before this laboratory was the search for and the study, mastering and application of the most effective existing spiritual practices for the benefit of the country. Special attention was paid to India and Tibet. Understanding the importance of the knowledge collected by the Barchenko Laboratory, SSSR's NKVD organized a similar, top-secret laboratory of their own. Unfortunately, the Barchenko Laboratory existed up until 1937. Even before the revolution, in 1905, while listening to a lecture by the professor of Roman Law A.S. Krivtzov, Barchenko got obsessed with the ideas of the Frenchman Saint-Yves d'Alveydre about an "Ancient Science" that comes from Shambala. Saint-Yves d'Alveydre had been initiated into ancient knowledge by Indian Brahmans. Even in the times prior to the revolution many educated Russians showed a profound interest in Saint-Yves d'Alveydre and remained in contact with him through their Russian wife, M. Keller and her son, the count A. Keller. After the Russian Revolution, Aleksander Barchenko also found out about Saint-Yves and the highly developed cosmic civilization of Shambala with its ancient knowledge. As a scientist, Barchenko was most attracted by the chance to establish contact with this civilization, in order to study their methods of universal scientific knowledge, which could aid humanity. Barchenko gave these universal science methods the Tibetan name "Dunkhor". This science, thought Barchenko, may give humanity – and first of all Russia – the key to solving social and economical problems, by means of taking possession of a hitherto unknown source of great cosmic powers.

And, despite Cosmoenergy being a method, which relies on the powers of the spiritual world, it is in many ways in agreement with the laws and concepts of modern-day physics. The common laws of human knowledge, which have manifested in the discoveries of quantum physics, for example, are not absolutely new: they had always existed in our culture and that which we see discovered today only works to support the wisdom of the ancient masters. There are grounds to suppose that it was in the top-secret laboratories that a method, which we now know as Cosmoenergy, was created based on the knowledge and technique brought over from Tibet, India, and places all over the world. The Roerich family played an important part in the development of this method.

During the years of the Russian Revolution, Nikolas Roerich immigrated with his family to the USA. In 1926, when he came from the US to Moscow, Nikolas Roerich conducted a series of intense negotiations with G.V. Chicherin, A.V. Lunacharsky and other Bolshevik leaders in order to gain their support for the realization of their grandiose plan of building a "country of the future", which would be very advanced. Nikolas wanted to realize this plan by means of the universal scientific knowledge from Shambala.

When the Roerich family went to Tibet, Nikolas Roerich really was invited to Shambala, where a deal was made with him that certain knowledge would be granted him. After this over the course of a long period of time, Nikolas Roerich received a representative of Shambala in their house, in the form of a person dressed in Buddhist robes, who gave him certain methods, techniques and knowledge, which later came to be known as Cosmoenergy. At that time, Nikolas Roerich's children were very young, but they were fascinated by the father's guest, and especially by how he would leave their house, as he never entered it through the door, appearing at once in their father's study. Every time he came, the session went deep into the night, and the children never saw how this Buddhist monk left their house.

Afterwards, Nikolas Roerich passed all of his knowledge on to his wife and children. Years later, one of Nikolas Roerich's sons Yuri returned to the Soviet Union and gave the secret service all of the knowledge and techniques his father had passed to him.

The Cosmoenergy method is not the invention of humans – even ingenious humans. Cosmoenergy is a method, which was given to humanity by a higher civilization. With the help of certain kinds of actions, Cosmoenergy allows us to use the rational forces of the Universe's non-material components, which we conditionally call "cosmic channels".

As modern-day science develops, we see an accumulation of scientific evidence supporting the existence of a person's "informational component". More and more often we see practicing doctors choose that methods of treating their patients that take into account the person's informational component; in particular, there are more and more specific and practical Cosmoenergy methods put into practice. We hope that this process will continue to be developed further.

BIOFIELD

DEFINITION OF BIOFIELD

The physical body of each human being consists of atoms, which, in turn, consist of protons and electrons. Each proton and electron has its own positive or negative charge. These charged particles are in a state of constant motion and, according to the laws of modern physics, thereby create various fields. Simply defined, the combination of these fields, created by the charged particles that make up a person's physical body, creates a person's "biofield".

Therefore, if each person's physical body is able to create its own biofield, it would then be completely logical to suppose that if a person's physical body has defects of some sort, these defects would then influence changes in the structure of their biofield. And vice versa – changes in the biofield may, with high probability, result in changes in the physical body. Thus, the physical body and its biofield are interconnected and do, in fact, influence each other.

BIOFIELD AND COULOMB'S LAW

As stated in Coulomb's law of physics, "the strength of a field is directly proportional to the magnitude of charge that has created this field and inversely proportional to the distance from a given point of the field to the source of the field squared". This formula allows the strength in any point in the field to be determined by a fraction with the magnitude of charge in the numerator and the square of the distance from a given point to the source of the field in the denominator. Thus, if the numerator and the denominator in this fraction both have numerical value, then no matter how great the distance between a given point and the source of the field may be, the result, however small it may be, will never be equal to zero.

According to Coulomb's law, even at a point that lies a great distance away from the source, the strength of the field it creates will not equal zero. Therefore, any electric field is infinite. Thus, it is natural to assume that there may indeed be a parallel between electric and bio fields, which are different but nevertheless similar in nature. Consequently, if a person's "biofield" is indeed in existence, then, by analogy with the electromagnetic field, it is most likely infinite.

BIOFIELD AND LAW OF QUANTUM PHASE TRANSITIONS

If, in accordance to Coulomb's law, the strength of the biofield decreases in opposite proportion to distance squared, it may also be presumed that, at certain field strength values, the law of quantum phase transitions will come into effect. Phase transition may be formulated as follows: "the change in quantitative characteristics of an element may lead to a sudden leap in its qualitative state". Philosophically speaking, this is known as the "transition from quantity to quality". We can see the quantum theory of "phase leaps" in everything around us: atoms, plants, animals, people, society, government, Earth, and Universe.

Looking at the continuous decrease in the force of the biofield in proportion to an increase in distance from the person's body can manifest the same quantum leap theory in a person's "biofield". The strength of the biofield decreases to a certain specific, critical amount at which the first quantum leap occurs. The segment of the biofield after the first quantum leap will be qualitatively different from the segment of the biofield before the leap.

The biofield segment before the quantum leap is called the "Etheric body", while the biofield segment after the first quantum leap is called the "Astral body". The intensity of the biofield continues a steady decrease until it reaches the intensity at which a second quantum leap occurs. The post-second quantum leap biofield segment is termed the "Mental body". At length, a third quantum leap occurs, the segment of the biofield after which is called the "Causal body". After the fourth quantum leap we come to the "True I body", and after the fifth quantum leap – the "body Absolute". Thus, the biofield can be seen to have a certain structure and to be composed of six "subtle bodies". These "subtle bodies" are as different from each other as, say, ice, water and steam - various phases that are still made up of the same elements.

BIOFIELD AND ITS SUBSEQUENT COMPONENTS

Upon analyzing the biofield's components, many researchers have noted the special, almost magical role played by the number three. According to several ancient teachings, a person's physical body is made up of three components: fire, wind and phlegm.

Modern-day conceptualizations allow us to divide a person's biofield into two equal parts, each of which consists of three components. The first half of the biofield, which consists of three subtle bodies: **the etheric, the astral** and **the mental**, directly makes up a person's **aura**. Similar to the physical body, a person's aura is material. The second half of the biofield, which also consists of three subtle bodies: **the causal body, the body of the true I, and the body of Absolute**, make up a person's **soul**, which is immaterial. Thus, a person is made up of two material components: their body and their aura, and one immaterial component – their soul. The soul, aura and physical body together make up a single whole – a person.

To reiterate – a person is made up of three main components: 1) the physical component (their physical body); 2) the energetic component (their aura); and 3) the soul, which contains information about the person's physical body and the processes therein.

The Universe also consists of three components: the **physical**, which includes all stars, planets, and nebulae; the **energetic** component – which includes light energy as well as the electromagnetic and other fields, and, thirdly, the **spiritual**, immaterial component—which, in turn, governs all the processes within the Universe. The spiritual component, or the spiritual world, if you will, refers to those rational powers that implement the actions necessary for processes in the Universe to go in a certain direction and in a certain way. These rational powers, or "minds of the spiritual world," differ from human minds, which are formed in the physical world.

Similar to the Universe, a person is made up of three parts – the physical, the energetic and the spiritual. The physical component is their physical body; the energetic component is their aura and the spiritual component – their soul. A person's spiritual component controls their physical body. A person's physical body is considered *alive* due to the presence of the spiritual component.

For the purposes of clarification, let's draw a comparison between a person and a computer. The computer, just like a person, also consists of three components: the physical (computer "hardware"), the energetic (it's power supply) and the spiritual (it's software and saved data). The physical and energetic components of a computer are obviously and tangibly material, while the computer's informational component is, in a certain sense, immaterial.

A person's spiritual component governs their physical body, making it *alive*. Under the guidance of the "control software," each organ in the physical body functions in a certain direction, specific to that organ, and accomplishes a specific task. The software programs within us control, regulate, direct and develop both the work of specific organs and systems and the workings of the body as a whole. The malfunction of any of the many programs leads to an aberration in the function of the corresponding organ. This leads to illness. A person develops certain health issues and illnesses as a result of the improper function of some of the programs in their spiritual component. We should still keep in mind, however, that these programs within a person's spiritual component are of a non-material nature.

A person's health is dependent on more than just the state of their spiritual component, i.e. the state of their soul; it is also dependent on the state of their aura. A person's aura holds all of the information regarding all of their deeds (actions, words, emotions, wishes, thoughts, etc.), which he has done and continues to do in this life, starting almost at birth, as *according to the principle of conservation, no human deed vanishes without a trace*, merely passing to another state of being – to another form of existence, i.e. into the aural. This allows us to view the aura as "a person's informational-energy biofield," in which the informational component is formed from their deeds, or actions, words, emotions, wishes and thoughts. The quality of "a person's informational-energy biofield" or, in other words, the state of a person's aura affects the person's physical body. The quality of the aura depends on the information it contains, and, in turn, the information contained by the aura comes about and collects as a result of the deeds of the given person, from birth on. If a person's aura is generally negative, there's nothing positive to be expected in terms of that person's physical health, as a "bad" or negative aura can only have a negative effect on a person's physical body. Thus, we see that a person's health is affected not only by the state of their spiritual component, formed by the collective experience of their past lives, but also by the state of their aura, which is being formed each day by the person themselves.

Yet another factor to be taken into account when discussing the health of an individual is their "internal energy" level, which is determined by the "charge", if you will, contained in the individual's "batteries". If a person's overall energy level is low, the person is hypotonic, as a result of which their organs and other various body systems work much less efficiently than they should. This leads to failures in the function of both specific organs and the organism as a whole. As a result of this, the body can no longer handle the various stresses it encounters and the person develops different health issues and illnesses.

When a person develops an illness, the cause of which lies in that person's spiritual component, for example, in the malfunction of the programs responsible for the health of the certain organs, then the help of those who can fix the malfunctioning programs is called for.

LAW OF CAUSALITY CONSERVATION (LAW OF KARMA)

According to this law, generalized and hence applicable to all occasions, not a single deed or action or word of a person, from the moment of their birth on, vanishes without a trace. Instead, they are reflected in their "Etheric body". The "Etheric body" contains all of the deeds performed by a person, both actions and words, in their present life. It follows from this that a person forms and influences the quality of their etheric body by the quality of their actions and words. The etheric body then influences the physical body (i.e. a person's health) correspondingly. So, we can see that what and how much a person sows with their actions and their words, that and that much he will correspondingly be reaping through their health, by means of the etheric body, as the etheric body and the physical body are interconnected and influence each other. This means that through their own actions and words, a person can either make their health better or make it worse. Not for nothing does the old saying go "Do unto others as you would have them do unto you."

A person's "Astral body" contains their emotions and desires. According to the principle of conservation, not a single emotion or a single desire a person has can vanish without trace; they unfailingly leave a trace in their "Astral body", explaining why the astral body is called the body of a person's emotions and desires. This leads us to the idea that a person's every emotion and desire, from birth on, do not simply vanish into thin air, but are reflected in their astral body. This, in turn, signifies that the quality of the astral body is determined by the person themselves, by means of the quality of their emotions and desires over the course of their entire life. The quality of these emotions and desires, manifested by the person over the course of their life, are reflected in the astral body, then, through the astral body, they will affect the person's health, and the person's health will, in turn, affect their fate and fortune. So, we can see that through their emotions and desires, which manifest as the astral body, a person can either improve or worsen their health.

A person's "Mental body" is the body of their thoughts. Not one thought a person thinks vanishes without trace; all of their thoughts are reflected in their "Mental body". Over the course of their entire life, practically from birth on, a person shapes the quality of their mental body via the quality of their thoughts. The mental body, in turn, has a direct affect on a person's health. What and how much a person sows with their thoughts, that and that much he will reap through their mental body in their health.

From this we can draw that a person's health is affected by their actions, words, emotions, desires and thoughts – through the etheric, astral and mental bodies, respectively. Together, these three bodies – etheric, astral and mental – make up a person's aura. Person's actions, words, emotions, desires and thoughts altogether can be called their *deeds*. It is through their deeds that a person can form and influence the quality of their aura. A person's aural quality is directly proportional to the effect it will have on the person's physical body. The principle of conservation is always at work, thus information concerning person's deeds does not disappear after the death of their physical body. This information enters another form of being – it transfers into a person's "Causal body".

After the death of the physical body, the influx of information into a person's etheric body regarding their actions and words stops. Without that informational component, the etheric body begins to break down. The information it contains, information regarding the person's actions and words over the course of their life, does not simply vanish without a trace – it gets transferred to the causal body, entering another plane of being. Similarly, according to the principle of conservation, the influx information into a person's astral body regarding their emotions and desires will also discontinue with their death. The lack of that informational source will cause the astral body to break down as well. But, with the breakdown of the astral body, all the information about person's lifelong emotions and desires contained therein does not vanish - it also gets transferred to the causal body. The same process occurs with the content of a person's mental body – their thoughts, collected over the course of their life, transfer to their causal body after their death. After a certain time has passed, all of the information about the person's deeds over the course of their life will have been transferred to the person's causal body. We should recall that a person's causal body is a component of their soul, which does not die with the death of a person's physical body.

Some believe that the soul is immortal – we will be more cautious and say that the lifespan of the causal body and of the other, more "ethereal" bodies, is significantly greater than that of the physical body. Thus, depending on the kind and quality of the deeds done by a person over the course of their life, their soul will be reincarnated in a new body, which, in accordance with the principle of conservation of cause and effect will be born in a certain time, in a certain place, to certain parents. And so the eternal, logical circle comes to completion – *what and how much a person has "sown" in their previous life, exactly that and so much shall they reap in the next*. The work of the aforementioned "channels" always proceeds in accordance to causal principle, or the law of cause and effect.

THE PERSON AND CHAKRAS

Ancient knowledge concerning chakras is the connecting thread between a person's physical body, their aura, their fortune and their soul. Chakras are impossible to define in any category of the sciences – physics or chemistry, psychology, physiology or any other science that is materialistic in nature. The word "chakra" itself means "wheel" in Sanskrit. In this context "wheel" signifies evolution: from one life to the next the apparatus governing man's physical body and the life of that body in the physical world undergoes improvement.

This governing apparatus (we can think of it as "packages of programs" similar to a computer) is an informational container of the "Mind of the Body" and "Mind of a Person" (see Appendices, Figure 18). "The Mind of the Body" is located in the main spinal cord. The "program packages" located in the spinal cord control, maintain, direct and develop each organ separately as well as the person's entire body. The "Mind of a Person" is located in the brain. These "program packages" allow the physical body to be alive and function, providing it with more comfortable medium for existence.

The spinal cord can be divided into five sections with a total of thirty-three vertebrae that make up the "Mind of the Body". The first section, the lowest, located in the coccygeal bone or the tailbone (the last four vertebrae), is the seat of the first chakra, or Muladhara in Sanskrit. The second section of the spinal cord, which consists of the five vertebrae of the sacrum, is the seat of the second chakra, or Swadhisthana in Sanskrit. The third section of the spinal cord located in the lumbar region - the small of the back made up of five vertebrae, is the seat of the third chakra, or Manipura in Sanskrit (navel chakra). The fourth section of the spine in the heart area of a person's spine consisting of twelve vertebrae is the seat of the fourth chakra, or Anahata in Sanskrit. Finally, the fifth section of the spinal cord consisting of seven vertebrae of the uppermost part of the spinal cord in the neck area is the seat of the fifth chakra, or Vishuddha in Sanskrit (throat chakra).

The "Mind of a Person" is located in the brain and associated with the sixth (Ajna) and seventh (Sahasrara) chakras. The Ajna chakra or the so-called 3rd eye is located between the eyebrows. The seat of the Sahasrara chakra is at the crown of the head in a person's brain.

1. MULADHARA CHAKRA

The first chakra is named Muladhara chakra in Sanskrit and referred to as the root chakra, as all of the other chakras are located above it. It is located at the base of the spine at the tailbone in back and the pubic bone in front. The first chakra is responsible for the health of the lower extremities (hips and legs), the lower part of the reproductive and digestive systems and prostate gland. It is also responsible for vitality, sleep and instincts. The first chakra contains all of the person's potential energy and holds the basic needs for survival, security and safety; thus, the condition of the first chakra determines a person's life, death and tonus.

The lowest chakra is the root of any growth and development, as well as a person's emerging realization of the divine nature of humans. A person with an active first chakra is a tireless worker who walks with a sure, firm gait. Such a person strives to extend their power, taking on the heaviest load they can possibly bear. When this chakra is blocked, a person may feel fearful, anxious, insecure and frustrated or experience problems like knee issues, obesity, anorexia nervosa, constipation, hemorrhoids, prostate problems, depression, asthenia, fatigue, irritability, weakness, a feeling of instability, anxiety, irrational fear, phobias, financial instability, greed, and selfishness.

During the recovery process of the first chakra, the following symptoms are possible: weakness in the legs and pain throughout the musculoskeletal system and the coccyx; sleepiness or, conversely, the shortening of sleep; mild depression, grief, self-pity: "What an unhappy and unlucky person I am!" jerking limbs, apathy, feeling hopeless.

2. SWADHISTHANA CHAKRA

The second chakra, if we count up from Muladhara chakra, is named Swadhisthana and referred to as the belly or sacral chakra. It is located two inches below the navel. Swadhisthana chakra is the center of reproduction, sexuality, self-confidence, strength of family relationships and children's welfare, intuition, creativity and emotions. The condition of this chakra correlates to a person's ability to procreate, relate to others in a friendly way and be creative. In terms of health, this chakra controls, supports, directs and develops the functionality of a person's urogenital system (women's sexual organs, kidney, bladder, ureters, urethra).

When this chakra is properly balanced, a person can express their emotions freely and relate to others well. When it is blocked, a person may feel emotionally manipulative, explosive, obsessed with sexual thoughts or experience problems like kidney weakness, constipation, still lower back, and muscle spasms, frigidity, infertility, sexual perversions, unhappiness in marriage, or diseases of the genitourinary system.

During the recovery process of the second chakra, the following symptoms are possible: lust, anger, greed, or aggravation of the genitourinary system diseases.

3. MANIPURA CHAKRA

The third chakra is named Manipura and referred to as the solar plexus chakra. It is located two inches below the breastbone in the center behind the stomach. This chakra is a repository of energy needed for life. It is the center of personal power, ego, passions, impulses, anger and strength. The state of Manipura chakra determines functioning of stomach, liver, gall bladder, pancreas, spleen, small intestine, as well as the state of a person's willpower, success, intelligence, and good luck in business. The state of Manipura chakra also determines a person's social and material state.

When this chakra is properly balanced, a person feels optimistic, friendly, outgoing, self-respecting, and expressive and has a strong willpower. When this chakra is blocked, a person may lack confidence, worry about other's opinions, be confused, feel that they are being manipulated by other people, feel depressed or experience problems like digestive issues, liver problems, diabetes, food allergies, nervousness, fears, mental illnesses and nervous exhaustion.

During the recovery process of the third chakra, the following symptoms are possible: various states resembling acute poisoning, temporary setbacks in business, feeling weak-willed, or change of work/occupation (always for a better job/position).

4. ANAHATA CHAKRA

The fourth chakra is named Anahata and referred to as the heart chakra. The fourth chakra is located behind the breastbone in front and on the spine between the shoulder blades in back. It is the center for love, compassion, family happiness, support, protection, and spirituality that directs a person's ability to love themselves and to give and receive love. It controls, maintains and helps develop the heart's ability to work, which is why the state of the fourth chakra determines the state of a person's heart and also lungs, circulatory system, thymus, shoulders, hands, and upper back.

When this chakra is balanced, a person feels compassionate, friendly, empathic, and nurturing towards others. When the heart chakra is blocked, a person may feel paranoid, envy, selfish, vain, indecisive, insensitive, clinging to people, sorry for themselves, afraid of getting hurt, or unworthy of love or experience problems like heart attack, bronchial asthma, hypertension, hypotension, insomnia, heart and lung diseases, and difficulties in breathing.

During the recovery process of the fourth chakra, the following symptoms are possible: palpitations, pain and constriction of the chest, shortness of breath, watery eyes, flashes of hatred, and problems in love relationships. If a spouse is a destructive obstacle in a person's life, there is a possibility of divorce.

The most important of all the chakras is the heart chakra. It affects a person's ability to love and express their love, both in relation to their close ones and to strangers. A person's capacity for growth and enlightenment is dependent upon the state of this chakra. Fear and reluctance to understand the other person is the main sources of many diseases, stress and suffering.

5. VISHUDDHA CHAKRA

The fifth chakra is named Vishuddha and referred to as the throat chakra. It is located in the collarbone at the base of the throat. The state of Vishuddha Chakra determines a person's sociability, creativity, communication abilities through thought, speech and writing, self-realization, and telepathic abilities. It supports throat, neck, teeth, ears, thyroid gland, and partially lungs and bronchi. The center of the Vishuddha Chakra is located at the base of the throat, which is why this chakra's state also determines a person's speech, the sounds they produce and their words.

When this chakra is balanced, a person communicates well, feels well balanced, and is inspired by art. When this chakra is blocked, a person may feel timid, week, unable to express their thoughts or experience problems like stuttering, sore throat, runny nose, inflammations, hyperthyroid, ear infections, and skin irritations.

During the recovery process of the fifth chakra, the following symptoms are possible: "cold without getting sick with cold", throat pain, sore throat, hoarseness, stuttering, tongue-tied, communication problems, quarrels, fights, and deterioration of relations with friends, relatives, co-workers.

6. AJNA CHAKRA

The sixth chakra is named Ajna Chakra (tricuta) and referred to as the third eye chakra. It is located between the eyebrows. Ajna Chakra is associated with the medulla oblongata and the pineal gland. It supports eyes, face, lymphatic and endocrine system, and brain. Ajna chakra is the center for intuition, psychic abilities, and receiving information about the multidimensional world.

When this chakra is balanced, a person is not afraid of death and not attached to material things. When this chakra is blocked, a person may feel non-assertive, be egotistical, afraid of success or experience physical problems like headaches, blurred vision, blindness, eyestrain.

7. SAHASRARA CHAKRA

The seventh chakra is named Sahasrara Chakra and referred to as the crown chakra. It is located at the crown of the head in the person's brain. The Sahasrara chakra is the center of spirituality, potential power of enlightenment, harmony of thought, and mental health.

When this chakra is balanced, a person has the ability to open up to the Divine.
When this chakra is blocked, a person may suffer from migraine headaches, nervousness, depression, or mental disorders.

INITIATION

"Initiation not only teaches us to be happy in this life, but also lets us die with hope."

(Cicero, Legibus, II, xiv, 36).

Initiation into the method of Cosmoenergy is given through the lineage of Teachers, a chain of continuous disciplic succession in the tradition of passing the Power and Knowledge from a Teacher to a student that is referred to as the parampara or "one by one" in the Vedas. The translation of the word "parampara" means "From the protected by Gods to the protected by Gods."

The true Knowledge and Power can be passed onto a disciple only from the one who is a part of this lineage of Teachers. Cosmoenergy, Yoga, Reiki, Ayurveda, Qigong, and a number of other practices are passed onto disciples by the parampara, though there are many other practices that do not have it. As the head of the Classic Cosmoenergy School Dr. Emil Bagirov says, "Before taking the Initiation into a doctrine, ask the teacher a question "Where is the parampara of this doctrine?" Only the one who has had a Teacher himself can become a Teacher.

The parampara of Cosmoenergy comes from the ancient Egypt, Tibet, India, North and South America where the initiated Teachers passed on their Power and Knowledge to the selected few. The secret knowledge, which nowadays is called Cosmoenergy, was passed on to Russia by the chain of succession through the Roerich family and has long been studied and researched in secret laboratories.

Over the years Dr. Emil Bagirov has conducted numerous treatment sessions, visited many countries, including Tibet and India, met with many worldwide recognized leaders of the well-known spiritual traditions, and received confirmation of the Divine origin, authenticity and purity of Initiations into Classic Cosmoenergy.

During the Initiation, the power of a Teacher is transferred to a student by the ordination of the Teacher, who themselves is a link in the chain of the parampara succession. Without the parampara, it is impossible to open the channels. The Initiation cannot happen without a Teacher who is an actual person in the flesh and not some astral spirit, or ghost, who appeared to a "contactee" and presented himself as a Teacher, God or whoever. The parampara is passed on only by the ordination of the living Teacher to their disciples.

The student must have an Initiation into a relevant practice. The Initiation serves as a spiritual protection of the parampara. The student must also have a firm intention to embark on the path of self-development and choose a Teacher with their heart and intuition. As the saying goes, "The Teacher comes when the student is ready." There is no competition among Teachers. Each student will be led to the Teacher who they have karmic ties to, i.e. to the Teacher the student deserves. Nothing is coincidental.

Students with Initiations to the parampara who keep contact with their Teacher will never lose the power of Initiations. In addition, by constantly working to assist their family members, relatives and everyone asking for help, the students will have more and more healing power.

The initiate is the person who took the first steps on their spiritual path and had their first spiritual insights, each of which is the key to more insights. Each expansion of consciousness, each rung of the ladder opens to the initiate the next step forward to be done by the initiate. Each initiation only shows even higher Initiations needed to be taken; and never comes a time when an aspirant (be it an average person, the initiate, or Teacher) remains static and is unable to progress further. Each major Initiation is merely a synthesis of small Initiations. Only by trying to expand their consciousness in the daily affairs of life, using the knowledge and techniques of the received knowledge, a student can hope to achieve the new stage, which is just the culmination of many previous ones. Only after receiving the initiation, the student enters into the stage of their self-development and begins to recognize the surrounding powers and influences.

The Cosmoenergy practitioner who took the Initiations does not need to change their position in the society. The only thing that is required of them is to follow the rules and methodology that was taught to them by their Teacher.

REASONS FOR GETTING INITIATED

Some of the reasons why a person should consider initiation into the channels, even if they are not planning to become a healer, include:

- **Protection**

  A person, like an antenna, receives different information and mental images from the outside world. Often the information received is negative which leads to depression, sudden mood changes, unfulfilled desires and obsessive behavior. This is not initiated by a person themselves, but is the result of external influences on a person. The more protection the person has, the more difficult it is for destructive, damaging and psychologically destabilizing information to affect the person. The protection, consequently, repels black magic attacks such as curses, the evil eye, damnation, etc.

- **Self-correcting the subtle body**

  Initiation into the channels permits the person to cleanse their own subtle body from the many negative influences received from the outside world, such as evil curses, the evil eye, jealous thoughts, negative wishes, damnation, bewitches, forced thoughts, vampirism, etc.).

- **Healing properties of the channels**

  The first channel the person will be initiated into is the Farun-Buddha channel, which has antioxidant properties. The Farun-Buddha channel aids cellular oxygen absorption and stabilizes intracellular metabolism. Regular application of the channel will reduce the risk of developing cancers.

- **Energy transformation**

  Every initiation into a channel will transform the subtle body by partially discharging accumulated negative karma and altering the vibration characteristics of their energy centers (chakras). This results in improved perception of positive information from the outside world, balancing the inner world and developing a philosophical view of life.

INITIATIONS INTO MASTER, ZOROASTRISM AND MAGISTER OF COSMOENERGY

After receiving initiations into at least 21 channels of the Buddhist and Magic groups consequently, the practitioner may receive initiation into Master of Cosmoenergy. The practitioner will receive the remaining 21 channels in one set over a course of three days. During the three-day initiation, the strength of the practitioner and each channel is increased. Each Master must have all 42 channels of both Buddhist and Magic groups of channels. Upon completion of the initiation, the practitioner becomes Master of Cosmoenergy.

As a second option, the practitioner may receive initiations into individual 42 channels of both Buddhist and Magic Channel groups consequently, adapt to new channels, and then receive initiation into Master of Cosmoenergy over a course of three days. There are no additional channels that are received during initiation into Master of Cosmoenergy, but the strength of the practitioner and each channel is increased. Upon completion of the initiation, the practitioner becomes Master of Cosmoenergy.

Initiation into Master of Cosmoenergy is performed over a course of three days:

1st day – fast before the first day of initiation

2nd day

3rd day – fast before the 3rd day of initiation, bring candles to the initiation

After receiving initiation into Master of Cosmoenergy, the practitioner opens the channels of the Buddhist group in the following way:

"Buddha, Buddha, otkrivayu kanali (dlia ochischeniya, lecheniya i zaschity), Buddha" "Farun-Buddha Firast, Farun-Buddha Firast, Farun-Buddha Firast"; "Farun-Buddha Shaon" (repeat 2-3 times); "Farun-Buddha Kraon" (repeat 2-3 times) and then all other compatible channels which are necessary for working with a patient. At the same time, the practitioner should imagine a light beam penetrating and covering them and the patient.

(The password translates as "Buddha, Buddha, I open channels for purification, healing and protection, Buddha: Farun-Buddha Firast, Farun-Buddha Firast, Farun-Buddha Firast"; "Farun-Buddha Shaon" (repeat 2-3 times); "Farun-Buddha Kraon" (repeat 2-3 times), etc.)

Next, the practitioner opens the channels of the Magic group compatible with the channels of the Buddhist group in the following way:

"Otkrivayu kanal [name of a channel]" (The password translates as "I open the channel [name of channel]) and repeat the name of a channel a number of times while imagining how the channel penetrates and covers them and the patient. For example, "Otkrivayu kanal Zevs, Zevs Zevs, Zevs..." and imagine how the channel penetrates and covers the practitioner and the patient. After opening the Zevs channel, the practitioner pronounces the password for opening the Tata channel "Otkrivayu kanal Tata, Tata, Tata..." while imagining how the channel penetrates and covers them and the patient.

Some channels of the Magic group are opened by mental visualization. These channels are used in the same way they were used before the practitioner became Master of Cosmoenergy.

WARNING! It is prohibited to use the passwords for opening the channels that the practitioner has not been initiated into and given permission to use by their Teacher.

After initiation into Master of Cosmoenergy, the practitioner may receive initiation into Zoroastrism channels that can be used during and after a standard treatment session. Initiation into **Zoroastrism** is performed over a course of three days. The practitioner should bring candles, matches and a glass or ceramic plate to the initiation.

1st day – fast before the first day of initiation (7 candles)

2nd day - (9 candles)

3rd day – fast before the 3rd day of initiation, bring candles to the initiation (11 candles)

After practicing for at least one year, the Master of Cosmoenergy may receive initiation into eight levels of **Magister of Cosmoenergy**. Each Magister channel is a synthesis of several channels. This is the reason why the channels of the Magister group are multi-level and possess high vibrational characteristics. The channels of the Magister group are used both for self-development and healing.

The Magister channels are compatible with the channels of the Buddhist and Magic groups and can be used both during and after a standard treatment session.

To use the Magister channels, the practitioner must receive three initiations with a one-month interval between them. The practitioner should fast for three days before each initiation and bring candles and matches to the initiation.

Level I Magister – the first initiation into Magister of Cosmoenergy. After the initiation, the practitioner becomes Level I Magister of Cosmoenergy, but cannot use the Magister channels yet.

Level II Magister – the second initiation into Magister of Cosmoenergy one month after the first initiation into Magister of Cosmoenergy. After the initiation, the practitioner becomes Level II Magister of Cosmoenergy, but cannot use the Magister channels yet.

Level III Magister – the third initiation into Magister of Cosmoenergy one month after the second initiation into Magister of Cosmoenergy. After the initiation, the practitioner becomes Level III Magister of Cosmoenergy. After the third initiation into Magister of Cosmoenergy, the practitioner may begin using the Magister channels. The Magister channels are compatible with the channels of the Buddhist and Magic groups and can be used both during and after a standard treatment session.

After receiving initiation into Level III Magister, the practitioner opens all channels of the Buddhist group as follows:

"Velikiy Buddha, otkrivayu kanali (dlya ochischeniya, lecheniya i zaschiti) Velikiy Buddha, Farun-Buddha, Firast, Shaon, Kraon, Svyatoi Moisei, ..." and so on until you open all necessary channels. (The password translates as " Great Buddha, I open channels for purification, healing and protection, Great Buddha: Farun-Buddha, Firast, Shaon, Kraon, Saint Moses, ...") While pronouncing the password, imagine a light flow covering you and the patient.

Then proceed to opening the channels of the Magic group:

"Otkrivayu kanal [name of channel]" (The password translates as "I open the channel [name of channel].) Repeat the name of a channel a number of times until you feel that the channel is open. While pronouncing the password, imagine a light flow covering you and the patient.

Then proceed to opening the Magister channels. The channels of the Magister group are opened with the Magic channel password: "Otkrivayu kanal [name of channel]" (The password translates as "I open the channel [name of channel].) Repeat the name of the channel a number of times until you feel that the Magister channel is open. While pronouncing the password, imagine a light flow covering you and the patient. Some Magister channels are opened with the mental image.

ATTENTION! It is prohibited to open channels without receiving initiation and permission from a Teacher!

To become a Teacher and teach the method of Classic Cosmoenergy by School by Emil Bagirov to others, the practitioner must receive five initiations into the highest Level VIII Magister of Cosmoenergy beginning with Level VI. Level IV Magister of Cosmoenergy can be received after a practitioner has worked with the Magister channels for at least three months. Initiations into Levels IV through VIII Magister of Cosmoenergy take place with a one-month interval between them. The practitioner should fast for three days before each initiation and bring candles and matches to each initiation.

Level IV Magister – the forth initiation into Magister of Cosmoenergy three months after the third initiation into Magister of Cosmoenergy. After the initiation, the practitioner become Level IV Magister of Cosmoenergy. After the fourth initiation into Magister of Cosmoenergy the practitioner receives the right to initiate and teach others the methodology of only three channels: **Farun-Buddha, Firast, and Zevs**. The practitioner's students can work with these channels on themselves and others. The Magister of Cosmoenergy automatically becomes the Progressor of Cosmoenergy when they began to initiate and teach the method of Cosmoenergy to others. After the fourth initiation, Level IV Magister of Cosmoenergy receives their cosmic name from their Teacher.

Level V Magister – the fifth initiation into Magister of Cosmoenergy one month after the fourth initiation into Magister of Cosmoenergy. After the initiation, the practitioner becomes Level V Magister of Cosmoenergy. After the fifth initiation into Magister of Cosmoenergy, the practitioner receives the right to initiate and teach others the methodology of all channels of the Buddhist group.

Level VI Magister – the sixth initiation into Magister of Cosmoenergy one month after the fifth initiation into Magister of Cosmoenergy. After the initiation the practitioner becomes Level VI Magister of Cosmoenergy. After the sixth initiation into Magister of Cosmoenergy, the practitioner receives the right to initiate and teach others the methodology of all channels of the Magic group.

Level VII Magister – the seventh initiation into Magister of Cosmoenergy one month after the sixth initiation into Magister of Cosmoenergy. After the initiation the practitioner becomes Level VII Magister of Cosmoenergy. After the seventh initiation into Magister of Cosmoenergy, the practitioner receives the right to initiate and teach others to be the Masters of Cosmoenergy.

Level VIII Magister – the eighth initiation into Magister of Cosmoenergy one month after the seventh initiation into Magister of Cosmoenergy. After the initiation the practitioner becomes Level VIII Magister of Cosmoenergy. After the eighth initiation into Magister of Cosmoenergy, the practitioner receives the right to initiate and teach others the methodology of Zoroastrism and to be the Magister of Cosmoenergy.

All training and initiations into this methodology should be received only from one Teacher. Receiving initiations from numerous different teachers obstructs the effectiveness of the method described in this book.

The schedule for receiving the initiations is not regulated, but dependent on the practitioner's decision; however, some of the initiations cannot be received earlier than the suggested timeframe.

Congratulations! You have completed your studies of the methodology of Classic Cosmoenergy School by Emil Bagirov.

METHODS OF PROTECTION

After initiation into the Farun-Buddha Universal Channel you will be able to heal yourself and any number of people. Work with one hundred percent confidence! Hundred percent confidence is in your awareness that you are working with the cosmic channels that are much bigger than you could ever imagine – it is "cosmic information". This "cosmic information" is not static or "thoughtless". By having doubts in the channels' power and capabilities you are programming yourself on making the doubts come true. You are not the Cosmos to doubt the Ability given to you. Having weaknesses and doubts you are interfering with actions of the "cosmic information". For example, you have a patient with a headache. If you think only for a moment that you are not able to help the patient or this will not work, you should not start the healing. Even if after the healing, the headache is gone, it will soon come back because you will not clean all negative "energy" (a cause of any pain is accumulation of negative "energy"). You should strive to understand what you are doing and how your action impact the environment. This understanding should be sensible and balanced.

You must strictly obey the rules of Protection and before you begin healing other people it is recommended to ensure your own protection first. The Initial point for building your own Protection will be the thought-form **"Protection"** you create.

The practitioner uses 3 means of protection: **the Shell, the Golden Pyramid,** and **the Channels.** Please note that the **Shell** protection can be used by the Practitioner only; other two means of protection (the Golden Pyramid and the Channels) may and should be used by the practitioner for their patients as well as for themselves.

The First Cosmic Law of Universe says: **"Visualizing means building." Building of protection** begins with visualizing it. After exercising the visualization of the protection for some period of time, it will eventually transform into the stable visual image, which will become the **permanent protection against negative influences** for the rest of your life.

You must start building your protection during the first week after initiation in the **Farun-Buddha** Universal Channel. It is meant to protect all of your seven energy centers (chakras).

It takes 14 days for the practitioner to build their protection. For the first 7 days you will be building the **Shell,** and for the next 7 days - the **Golden Pyramid**. The "building" procedure has to be done 4 times a day (in the morning, in lunch time, in the evening and before going to bed). You have to stand relaxed, preferably with closed eyes, for 10 minutes each time. To avoid distraction from outside noise you may listen to some slow music with no words.

1. The Shell

You have to imagine yourself inside an elongated shell (similar to the mussel shell). Imagine that the Shell is hollow and its inner walls are smooth, clean and of mother-of-pearl color (see Appendices, Figure 1). The outside walls of the shell are grey and rough. The shucks of the shell are closed behind your spine and are open in front of your face. The length of the shell should be as follows: 30-40 cm above your head and including your knees at its lower end. The shucks should not be narrow so that no part of your body is exposed. The Shell should fit your body constitution. If the Shell is too small, it will be too tight, if it is too big, it will be too heavy for you. Other dimensions of the Shell should be the following: 20 cm from your shoulders and 50 cm in front of your body. There should be 50 cm from the shell to your spine, so that you feel comfortable inside the shell.

While "building" the Shell you have to do the following exercise: imagine that the shucks of the Shell open and close slowly, then open the shucks and shut them sharply. If during shutting of the shucks, you feel that your shoulders moved forward, as if being pushed by the shucks (though in reality, your shoulders remained still), it means that you managed to "build" the mental image of the Shell correctly. The shucks of your Shell will remain slightly open most of the time, but they will shut when you need protection. In the future your Shell will shut its shucks on its own to protect you in case if you are to be exposed to any negative influences.

In addition, while "building" the Shell, you should do the following exercise during the day: For example, in the morning after "building" the Shell, you are going somewhere and notice that a passing-by person is looking at you. You should continue where you were going, but imagine your Shell that is built into your body and close its shucks. Keep going with the shucks of the Shell closed as long as the person is looking at you. When the person passes by and does not look at you any more, you can open the shucks of the Shell.

After 7 days of visual "building" of the Shell, it will "root" itself into your shoulders and you will not need to "build" it anymore. It will be in your memory almost for the rest of your life. Why for the rest of your life? For example, when you are asked to memorize a poem in a short time, you can learn and forget about it quickly. However, when you spent several days memorizing it, it will stay in your memory longer. The same idea is with the Shell. Our memory is located in our sub-consciousness, which penetrates everywhere and knows everything about everything. If someone is influencing you from somewhere, your sub-consciousness will know about it and close the Shell, because the information about the Shell that you built is in your sub-consciousness. The Shell will not let in any influence on you. Thus, when somebody is looking at you, you should close the Shell, because somebody's gaze is an invisible energetic influence. The Shell will not let in even the smallest influence on you non-stop around the clock because our sub-consciousness, in contract to our consciousness, never shuts off. Thus, the earlier you begin building your protection, the better it is for you.

In the future you will only need to "check" the Shell at least once a month, though it would be better if you "have a look" at your protective Shell once a day. Until the Shell is not grown into your body, you have to think about it and train it. For example, if someone looked at you badly, you should shut the Shell. In the future your Shell will work in auto-mode and will shut itself whenever it is necessary. The Shell lets positive energy go through to the inside. No energy can destroy your Shell. Moreover, the bigger some energy influence on the Shell is, the thicker your Shell's shucks become. You will notice the extra weight when shucks of your Shell become thicker. The Shell cannot be built for the patients.

2. Golden Pyramid

Imagine a square sheet of gold 10-15 cm below the First Chakra. Then imagine the peak of the Pyramid about 30-40 cm above your head, imagine the golden sides or edges of the Pyramid sloping down from the peak to the base of the Pyramid (see Appendices, Figure 2). The size and proportions of the Pyramid are individual for each practitioner. Your sub-consciousness that knows what is better for you will help finish building the Pyramid.

After you visualize the Pyramid for 10 minutes 4 times a day for 7 days it will root into your Shell and remain there forever. Protective properties of the Golden Pyramid and the Shell do not interact. The Golden Pyramid can also be built for your patients. You have to "check" your protection in the beginning. Ideally built protection will guard you against any negative energy influence/attacks.

The Golden Pyramid cannot be controlled; therefore, it could be built for other people. You can take a photograph of a person who cannot come to the session (black-and-white or color photograph, full height or half-height or only a face). While looking at the photo, mentally build the image as if this person is not just a mental image, but as if they are standing in front of you, so that there is no difference for you.

3. Channels

The channels also have protective functions. Practitioners are always under influence of the channels and if there is any negative energy attack their protection will be activated automatically.

You may use the channels whenever you think about them. This will be the "non-professional use" of the channels. The channels may be used at any time of the day, any number of times and in any place (you can open the channels while walking, cleaning, reading, etc.).

Note: It is important to remember that your protection may weaken under the influence of negative emotions, including fear. You must **control your emotions and actions**. You may think about other people's problems and feel for them but don't let the feelings inside you. This may affect your Protection. Everything we do (all our actions) affects our Protection too. Striking examples of a "wrong behavior" could be our vanity or temptation. Practitioner practicing Cosmoenergy is no better or above other people, they are just in the possession of the Knowledge. The main goal of any practitioner's self-discipline should be control over their thoughts, words, actions, emotions and feelings, ethics and respectful attitude towards everyone and everything and maintaining a neutral position.

NON-PROFESSIONAL USE OF CHANNELS

For non-professional use of the channels, the practitioner should follow the rule: "Open the channel as soon as you remembered about it" (but no earlier than an hour after opening it previously). The use of channels in such a way is possible any time of the day, any number of times and at any place. For example, if you remembered about a channel during performing some daily task, it is necessary to open it. If you remembered about it during a walk or while driving, immediately open the channel without halting your activity.

To understand the necessity of following this rule, it is necessary to know that during the Initiation into a specific channel, the information about the channel appears in your sub-consciousness. Each use of the channel leads to solidifying of this information in the sub-consciousness, therefore, with time, the sub-consciousness will know that you have a channel with specific characteristics, which is available for your usage. When you feel some negative influence, your sub-consciousness will throw the information about a channel into your consciousness and all of a sudden you will remember about the channel. Thus, the rule "remembering about the channel" means that your sub-consciousness considers it necessary for you to open the channel on yourself at that exact moment when you need it because your sub-consciousness is a part of your biofield, which penetrates everywhere and knows everything about everything, including when you will be under the negative influence. This is the reason why you should follow this rule.

For non-professional use of channels, it is recommended to open the channels for protection in the morning immediately after waking up and at night before bedtime. You can build protection by opening the channels for yourself, any other person or a group of people. The channels can be opened simultaneously on yourself and the people who need protection. When opening the channels, use only the password described in a specific channel and imagine the channel as a flow of light which at first covers you (beginning above your head and ending below your feet) and then the patient (beginning above their head and ending below their feet).

PROFESSIONAL USE OF CHANNELS

For professional use of the channels the practitioner should follow a standard treatment session procedure. During the "no-contact" sessions, the practitioner does need to perform the paragraph 5 of the standard treatment session procedure or perform only the sub-paragraph 5.1 ("writing-off"). Paragraph 8 is performed with semi-contact method or mentally. During contact treatment sessions, all paragraphs of the standard treatment session are performed.

STANDARD TREATMENT SESSION PROCEDURE

1. Ask your patient(s) to stand in a relaxed position with their eyes closed.

2. Open the channels.

3. Open the patient(s) in the following order:
   - Lotus
   - Shoulders
   - Chest
   - Abdomen
   - Back
   - Hands
   - Feet

4. Open the Well

5. Practitioner's work with the patient(s):

   5.1 "Writing off" problems

   5.2 Work with chakras

   5.3 Work with problem

   5.4 Miscellaneous

6. Close the Well.

7. Close the patient(s).

8. Enlarge and align the patient's Aura.

9. Thank the Channels. Ask the patients to open their eyes.

The session is now finished.

FULL PROCEDURE OF THE STANDARD TREATMENT SESSION

The practitioner should always work with their eyes opened. It is necessary to always cleanse the premise where the standard treatment session is held with the Firast channel before the session is commenced. During the standard treatment session, the practitioner should open and work with the channels silently without disturbing the patient.

1. Ask patient(s) to stand in the relaxed position with their eyes closed

Before starting a standard treatment session, it is necessary to explain to your patient(s) what they are supposed to do during the session. It is important that the patients are standing straight during the session as the human's energy-system is set up in a vertical order. Patient have to stand relaxed but straight and symmetrically, however, the patient may move their body (for example, dance, sway to the sides, bend down, etc.). The patients should NOT stand on one side, bend one knee, or cross legs or arms as this will obstruct effective extraction of negative energy from the patients' bodies and, correspondingly, prevent from proper healing and positive corrections in their lives.

Patients have to keep their eyes closed during the whole course of the treatment session. This is necessary in order to have access to the patients' mental bodies. Mental body is the inhabitation area for our thoughts, and our thoughts are the initial source of everything that happens in our lives. That is why, first of all, it is important to work on improving the quality of our thoughts. This will plant seeds of positive changes in our lives and allow us in the future to avoid the negative events that made the patients seek help of practitioners.

The patients' eyes should be closed in order to minimize distraction caused by any outside sounds and noise. Patients should not think about anything in particular, (i.e. should not do any mental work).

During the treatment session patients should be fully relaxed. There could be some sensations inside the patient's body and mind or color pictures/visions flicks in front of their closed eyes, (i.e. each patient should fully concentrate on themselves and theirs own sensations).

The treatment always causes liberation of negative energy from the patients' bodies. This may reveal itself in headaches, increased heartbeat, dizziness, etc. If this happens, the patient may sit down on a chair (which should be located behind each patient) without asking the practitioner's permission, but should keep their eyes closed all the time. After the patient gets better they have to stand up again (after the patient sits down and begins to feel better, they should again stand up because the channels' influence significantly decreases when the patient is not standing).

If necessary, the patient can briefly leave the room. After they are back, the practitioner can continue working with the patient from the point when the session was interrupted.

2. Open the channels

The practitioner should open the channels on themselves and, then on their patients, i.e. the practitioner has to pronounce the password for opening the necessary channels and visualize how the channels pass through and cloak the bodies of the practitioner and the patients (see Appendices, Figure 3).

If the practitioner uses a few channels during the treatment session, they have to open and visualize them one by one, i.e. pronounce the password and imagine how one channel passes through and cloaks the bodies of the practitioner and the patients, then do the same with the second channel, then the third channel and so on.

When using the healing channels; DO NOT additionally set an objective for the channels to implement a certain task or treat certain body organs because the channels are much more intelligent than people. The channels will themselves identify each patient's problems and work with them. The practitioner's thoughts and objectives will only interfere with the channels' work.

3. Open the patient(s)

1) Lotus

Lotus is the 7th chakra. Different theories mention different number of petals in a Lotus flower, but it is not important for practitioners, as we are only working with sepals (which form the outer protective layer in a bud). Lotus always has 4 sepals. To open the Lotus, you have to imagine how you are opening 4 sepals of the Lotus. You can also open and close the Lotus with your eyes.

You should open the Lotus during each treatment session, except when you need to overload the patient's aura with the channel(s) (i.e. when trying to increase the patient's aura, the Lotus should be closed). Do not worry about over-loading the patient's aura too much, because the Lotus is working as a valve and will release the excess energy out.

To open the patient's Lotus, visualize that there is the Lotus flower on the top of the patient's head. Imagine that the Lotus flower consists of 4 petals and the petals are closed. Visualize that you are opening the petals as follows: the left and the right petals open aside and the front and back petals open forward and backwards, correspondingly (see Appendices, Figure 4). If you cannot do this (open the Lotus) mentally, imagine that you are doing this with your hands.

2) Shoulders

Visualize that there are epaulettes on the patient's shoulders. Imagine that you unbutton the epaulettes from the throat outwards.

3) Chest

Visualize that there is a beam of light coming from your eyes or from the fingers of your right hand. Imagine that the beam cuts the patient's chest (from the throat down) and then you need to open the edges of the cut like sliding a door.

4) Back

If the patient has problems with their respiratory system or with the spine then you have to open the patient's back in the same way as the chest.

5) Abdomen

Cut the patient's abdomen with the beam of light coming from your eyes or fingers and open the edges of the cut like sliding doors.

6) Hands

One by one cut the patient's hands vertically into two parts and open the parts so that there is a crack between them.

7) Feet

One by one cut the patient's feet into two parts and open them so that there is a crack between the two parts of each foot. If you have a few patients during the session, you have to open them one by one, i.e. open Lotus, shoulders, chest, abdomen, hands and feet on one patient then do the same on another patient and so on.

4. Open the Well

There are two types of the Well:

- The Well to be opened during a standard treatment sessions:

    This Well is to be opened for the whole room where the session is conducted. To open this Well, you need to visualize the floor in the room as the lid of the Well that you are sliding out. The depth of the Well is towards the centre of the Earth. If you look inside the Well, you will not see the bottom because the grayish mist obscures it. Set an objective "Everything that goes into the Well will be processed and then improve fertility of Earth".

    Note: In cases when you have a hypotensive patient, you need to put the patient with low blood pressure separately in the corner of the room and not open the well underneath him. The well is a very powerful tool for withdrawing (drawing down) energy, that is why the hypotensive patient should stay in the corner and the practitioner should not have an open well underneath them.

- The Well to be opened when using "Motor-Well" method (not during standard treatment sessions):

Visualize a sewer manhole in the spot on the floor/ground where you need to have the Well for pulling out the negative energy using the "Motor-Well" method. Imagine that you removed the lid from the manhole and put it aside and that there is the Well under the lid. Then imagine early morning light white fog inside the well. You must know that the Well is deep and stretches to the center of the Earth, but you cannot see the bottom as it is obscured by grayish mist. Set an objective "Everything that goes into the Well will be processed for improving fertility of Earth".

5. Work with the patient (s)

Paragraph 5.1 "Writing off" problems

The "writing off" of a certain problem means taking this problem off a patient, writing the problem down on a piece of paper, and then eliminating it by means of fire. Why do we do problem's "write offs"? We do this in order to alleviate some of the negative aspects in the patient's life, making them easier to deal with and less painful. By doing the "writing off" procedure for our relatives and friends every day, we can help make their life much easier. You can do "write offs" at any time during the day, but it is better to do it in the course of a healing session with your patient. On days when you are not doing healing sessions, the "writing off" procedure can be done in the early morning. If you can't do it in the morning or at all that day, don't worry – just do it when you have the chance. The "writing off" procedure will be much more effective if you do it while the patient is standing under the channels you opened for them.

Always remember that during any healing you do, you must open the channels not just for the patients you are working with, but for your own protection as well. Take a piece of paper and draw one five-point star (pentacle) in the middle of the left side of the paper and one in the middle of the right side, staying as close to the left and right edges as you can, so that one of the peaks of each pentacle touches the corresponding edge (see Appendices, Figure 5). By doing so, you create an energy corridor between yourself and your patient in order to minimize any interference during the "writing off" process. Place the piece of paper on a hard surface, so that the images from your paper are not accidentally copied onto any other surface. Then, looking at your patient, start drawing figure eights (sideways infinity signs) and let your hand continue to draw them without stopping, staying within the pentacles. Concentrate on your goal to write off a certain problem of the patient. Switch off your consciousness and continue to monotonously draw the same figure eights, starting at the top of the page with the pentacles. If you keep drawing the same signs over and over, for some period of time, the infinity signs will change their shape and transform into different signs, shapes, symbols, or even words. This means that your arm is now driven by your subconscious mind, which then allows you to transfer the patient's problem onto the paper.

Do not draw over the pentacles, or in the same area where you have already drawn something. Direct your arm down and draw in the blank area on the piece of paper. Glance at the paper occasionally just to see if you are drawing in the blank area. If there is no blank space left on the paper and you still feel that your arm needs to continue drawing, you should fold the piece of paper so that the writing is inside (but don't look at what you drew and don't try to remember what the drawings look like), then take a blank piece of paper, draw the pentacles on its sides and continue drawing the figure eights. It may take several pieces of paper until you feel that your arm has stopped drawing. Put the used pieces of paper (folded with the information side in) aside, but not on the pile of blank paper. When your sub-consciousness stops driving your arm and your arm stops drawing, the "writing off" is complete, i.e. you have transferred the patient's problem onto the paper. The process of "writing off" a particular problem may take up to 10 minutes for a single patient.

After you have stopped writing the problem off, you must burn all the used paper immediately. It is best to burn the paper in another room, because it will give off foul-smelling acrid smoke. When burning the paper, mentally state the following: "I wish to burn the patient's problem along with this paper, and all that has been burnt will benefit the Earth, making it more fertile."

All the paper should be burnt to ashes; no single piece should be left, however small. If some small piece of paper is left, you should burn it, along with another piece of paper. Then throw the ashes out the window or flush them down the toilet.

The problems you are writing off are nothing more than dirty energy, and dirty energy is a lie, so we transfer it onto paper and set it on fire. Truth is eternal and it cannot be destroyed by fire, nor by anything else.

After burning the problem you have "written off" from one patient, you may start the same procedure for the next patient and then immediately burn the used paper as well. The "writing off" procedure for the same patient should be done no more than once a day. If a patient sees several different Cosmoenergy practitioners, the practitioners have to agree amongst themselves who's doing the writing off procedure today, who's doing it tomorrow, etc. One must never do the "writing off" procedure for oneself. By writing off other people's problems, you will, indirectly, also be working on your own problems.

When you are doing the "writing off" procedure during a standard treatment session with the patient, it is helpful to visualize the dirty, heavy energy flowing down into the well you have opened in the floor from various cuts and lesions (imagined) on the body of the patient.

Illnesses, such as asthma and diabetes, occur as a result of so-called "necrotic connections" (mental or emotional connections to/with people who have died). In order to treat these illnesses, we need to remove the connection between the patient and the dead. Here's how we do this: Place two photographs (one of your patient's and one of the deceased person with whom they still have a connection) in front of you and do the "writing off" procedure mentally stating your goal: "I want to remove the necrotic connection between these two people." Continue with the "writing off" procedure until your hand stops drawing, but do not exceed 10 minutes. Perform the "writing off" procedure for this "necrotic connection" during the course of the patient's treatment as many times as your intuition tells you to. Your intuition will let you know when the "necrotic connection" is removed.

Paragraph 5.2 Work with Chakras

Healing of any illness has to be started from purifying/activating the chakras. Practitioners can work with the first five chakras only.

The first chakra, called Muladhara, is the lowest chakra. It is located in the base of the spine – near the tailbone.

The second chakra, called Swadhisthana, is located a bit higher than Muladhara – approximately over the pubic bone.

The third chakra, called Manipura, is located on the level of the belly button.

The fourth chakra, called Anahata, is located in the middle of the chest – on the level of the heart.

The fifth chakra, called Vishuddha, is located in the base of the neck. Practitioners are NOT allowed to work with the sixth and the seventh chakras.

The sixth chakra, called Ajna (also called "The Third Eye"), is located between the eyebrows.

The seventh chakra, called Sahasrara (also called "The 1000-petalled Lotus") is located on the crown of the head. **Attention!** The sixth and the seventh chakras should never be cleansed or activated!

You can restore the chakras' activity using either the Farun-Buddha channel or a combination of the Farun-Buddha, Firast and Zevs channels (if the practitioner has been initiated into these channels).

To restore the chakras' activity, you should:

• Approach the patient from the right-hand side and place your hands over the patient's first Chakra. Your right hand is placed over the chakra from the patient's front side and your left hand is placed parallel to the right hand from the patient's rear side. The Chakra is visualized as a golden ball between your hands (see Appendix, Figures 6 and 7).

• Imagine the Farun-Buddha channel or three channels Farun-Buddha, Firast and Zevs (if the practitioner has been initiated into these channels) being transmitted from the palms o your hands onto the chakra which is visualized as a golden ball between your hands and utter th names of all three channels in any sequence, imagine how the golden ball heats up and begins t boil. This indicates that the chakra has been purified. The golden ball serves the practitioner a an indicator of how long they should work with the chakra. If you only have the Farun-Buddh channel, utter many times "Farun-Buddha, Farun-Buddha, Farun-Buddha", etc. If you have th Farun-Buddha, Firast and Zevs channels, utter:

"Farun-Buddha, Farun-Buddha, Farun-Buddha; Farun-Buddha-Firast, Farun-Buddha Firast, Farun-Buddha-Firast, Firast, Firast, Firast; Zevs, Zevs, Zevs";

again:

"Farun-Buddha, Farun-Buddha, Farun-Buddha; Farun-Buddha-Firast, Farun-Buddha Firast, Farun-Buddha-Firast, Firast, Firast, Firast; Zevs, Zevs, Zevs";

and again:

"Farun-Buddha, Farun-Buddha, Farun-Buddha; Farun-Buddha-Firast, Farun-Buddha Firast, Farun-Buddha-Firast, Firast, Firast, Firast; Zevs, Zevs, Zevs" (until the practitioner feel their hands are warm)

at the end imagine that the golden ball is boiling and repeat many times "Zevs"

then repeat many times "Farun-Buddha-Firast, Farun-Buddha-Firast, Farun-Buddha Firast, Firast, Firast, Firast";

finally repeat "Farun-Buddha" many times.

• Precede in the same manner with the second, third, fourth (where the hands are place crosswise) and fifth chakras.

While working with the fourth chakra the practitioner's hands are turned in a way tha they form a cross. The practitioner's left hand stays in the horizontal position behind the patient' back and their right hand is in a vertical position in front of the patient, i.e. the practitioner need to turn their right hand so that their four fingers are directed up and the thumb is turned aside The thumb is underneath the patient's chest so that the chest (or the breast) is over th practitioner's thumb (see Appendices, Figure 8). While holding their hands in this position, the practitioner should then utter the names of the channels in any sequence.

If during your work with a chakra, it does not get activated, it means that that the chakr contains too much "dirty energy". In this case, you should remove the "dirt" by using th "Motor-Well" method. Then work with the chakra as described above.

"Motor-Well" Method

"Motor-Well" method is used for removing "dirty energy" from the patient's body (for example, pain/aches, headache and "dirty energy" in the chakras).

"Dirty energy" in the person's body can cause not only discomfort, but also pain. For example, concentration of "dirty energy" in the person's head causes headache. The reasons for this could be:

1. Head injuries
2. Inflammation

There are two types of "dirty energy" – light and heavy. The light "dirty energy" makes the person lighter, and the heavy "dirty energy" makes the person heavier. The more amount of heavy "dirty energy" the person has, the more it pulls them down. This can be tested by an electronic scale – weigh a patient before and after a standard treatment session. The difference in weight will help illustrate to the patient the effectiveness of Cosmoenergy. The Channels not only heal, but also cleanse the person from the negative "energy". The more negative energy left the person, the lighter the person will be, and if there is a lot of light "energy", the person will be heavier. There are thousands of such researches that were conducted. If a person comes to you for the first time, the difference in weight before and after the session could be in kilograms, and after attending several sessions – in grams.

The reason for light "dirty energy" is alcohol intoxication. When a person drinks alcohol, it goes to blood and causes red blood cells to begin gluing to each other forming clusters and blood clots. The more the person drank, the more blood clots are formed. The clots "walk around" blood and eventually get to the brain. The brain's cells feed capillaries. If the clot gets to capillaries, it will clog the capillary so the blood does not get to the brain causing the cells to die. The cells dissipate forming light "dirty energy". The more alcohol the person drank, the more amount of light "dirty energy" they have. That is why in the morning, the person has a headache and light "dirty energy" strives to the top, filters through and leaves. And if there is heavy "dirty energy", for example, due to a head injury, heavy headache appears, but it is striving to the bottom of the person's body; however, leaves the person's body through the head and the headache goes away but not for a long time. Heavy "dirty energy" goes up and down and when it gets to the head, the headache will repeat. It is called chronic pain, and it can continue for decades. With the method of "Motor-Well," you can help the person get rid of their chronic headaches once and for all.

To work with the "Motor-Well" method, make the patient sit on a chair (do not open the well underneath him), approach them from the left with your right side and put your right hand on the patient's fontanel – the first position of your hand. The right arm should be completely straight, and the palm should be parallel to the floor. Then under your left palm open a "well" by imagining a sewer manhole, mentally opening the lid of the sewer manhole and imagining a well going deep to the center of Earth with a blue-grey smoke inside. Set an objective – "Everything that goes there will be recycled and used by Earth." The "well" is the same as the one that you open during a standard treatment session, but of different size. Open the "well" and imagine a "tube" inside your arms going through both your left and right arms. The arms should be on the same line, otherwise, the "tube" will be curved and the "pump" will not work correctly. Then imagine a "motor" inside your right shoulder and while maximally flexing your right arm, switch on the "motor". Thus, a "pump" is formed which sucks the "dirty energy" from the patient's fontanel through the "tube" to the "well" to the centre of Earth. Then look under your left palm, not with your eyes, but with your inner vision, and begin to imagine a stream of black color, wherein not forgetting to flex the left arm because the more you flex it, the more powerfully will the "motor" work (see Appendices, Figure 9). After some time you will see that the color of the stream became lighter, changing from black to grey, then to light grey, and finally, to transparent color. When you see a transparent stream, it means that all "dirty energy" has been removed from the patient's fontanel.

The second position of your hand: place the right palm on the crown of the patient's head and pull all "dirty energy" until the stream changes color from black to transparent. Repeat the same procedure on the third position of your hand – place your right palm on the patient's nape (back of the head), fourth position - your right palm is on the back of the patient's neck, fifth and sixth positions – your right palm is on the left and right temples. The patient should lean their head to the left and you can put your right palm on their right temple. Repeat the same procedure with the left temple. After the sixth position, close the "well" by imagining a thicker lid that closes the sewer hole. The seventh position – stand with your right side facing the patient and placing your right palm on the patient's forehead. Open the second "well" under your left palm; again imagine a "tube", a "motor" inside your right shoulder and maximally flexing your right arm, pull "the dirty energy", switch on the "motor" which will work until the stream becomes transparent.

The same method can be used to help a person with an injury (cut, bump, strain, etc.) if medical assistance is not required, regardless of how old the injury is. If it is a fracture or dislocation, medical assistance is required.

For removing pain, you have to stand with your right side to the patient, place your right palm to the affected area and pull out the pain with the "motor" through the "tube" into the "well."

For purifying chakras, you have to stand with your right side to the patient, place your right palm on the front of the patient's chakra and pull out "dirty energy" with the "motor" through the "tube" into the "well."

Notes:

1. You have to be clearly aware where all the chakras are located to accurately place your palms over each chakra. You have to work with one hundred percent confidence. This objective will help your sub consciousness to control your internal vision and direct your hands accurately over each chakra. When doing this, you should have NO doubts that you are doing it correctly.

Your right hand is a working hand, and it should always be in front of the patient while your left hand should be behind the patient. When you begin working with each chakra, mentally set a dual objective - "I would like to see and put my hands over the 1st, 2nd, etc. chakra". Then work with each chakra as described above.

2. If you cannot activate some chakras with the Farun-Buddha, Firast and Zevs channels, it means that the chakra is badly contaminated. In this case, the chakra should first be cleansed with the "Motor-Well" method described above and then again treated with the three channels (Farun-Buddha, Firast and Zevs). If purifying the chakras using the three channels does not bring the expected healing results, you may use the Titan channel. The Titan channel is used in exceptional cases only. If you use the Titan channel for purifying chakras, you should not apply other channels to the chakras at the same time. The only exception to this rule is when you treat heart disease (it does not matter which one). In this case, you should purify and launch the fourth chakra as follows: begin with Titan, then apply Zevs, then Firast and finish with the Farun-Buddha channel. No other channels, except for these four may be applied to the chakras.

3. The Shaon channel works with chakras independently, (i.e. without our assistance and without close contact of our hands to chakras.)

4. If you visualize chakras in some color, other than gold, you cannot be sure if the chakras were fully cleared (of dirty energy), because you will still be able to see the color, but you will not see what's inside the chakra. That is why we are using the method of golden chakras. This method helps us develop our visualization skills.

5. Do not leave an arc on chakras.

6. Treatment of all illnesses should be commenced with purifying chakras and restoring overall patient's energy level.

Paragraph 5.3 Work with problems

In paragraph 5.3 of the standard treatment session procedure, you can work on various patients' problems, for example, their internal organs and removing pain/problem using the "Motor-Well" method. When working with internal body organs and removing pain/problem (for example, removing salt deposits, stones, sand, tumors, pain, you should apply arcs to the patient's affected area by:

1. Standing to the right from the patient, placing the right hand on the front of the patient's affected area and pulling the "dirty energy" from the affected area using the "motor-well" method through the left hand into the open "well."

2. Making an "energy drain" by mentally imagining a ray coming from your finger or eye, cutting the affected area with the ray crosswise, mentally opening the corners of

the cut, imagining a drain tube placed in the center of the cut, closing the corners of the cut to keep the tube in place and mentally looking at it for 10 seconds so that the tube stays in the affected area (see Appendices, Figures 10 and 11). The drain is necessary for the negative energy to leave through the tube.

3. Standing to the right from the patient and placing the right hand on the front of the patient's body and the left one on the patient's back with the affected area staying between your hands, uttering the name of the channel any number of times (for example, Farun-Buddha Shaon, Farun-Buddha Shaon, Farun-Buddha Shaon, Shaon, Shaon, Shaon, etc.) while imagining the channel being transmitted between your palms to the affected area forming the arc stretching outside the boundaries of your palms until you can mentally see the arc and your palms begin to feel warm, removing your hands, and leaving the arc on the affected area (see Appendices, Figure 12).

Note: Prior to the treatment session, open the Midi channel (if you have been initiated into the Midi channel) and look through the patient's whole body to determine which bodily organs you should treat and which channels you should use during the session.

Paragraph 5.4. Miscellaneous

In paragraph 5.4 "Miscellaneous", you can work on various tasks, for example:

Cleansing the patient's head

It is recommended to cleanse the head of all patients during each standard treatment session. If you only have the Farun-Buddha channel, you can cleanse the patient's head using the "Motor-Well" method (see above). If you have the Farun-Buddha, Firast and Zevs channels, you can cleanse the patient's head by:

1. Standing behind the patient, hold your hands in a shape of a boat, palms facing up below the patient's head at the neck level near the patient's body while avoiding contact with the patient's body (see Appendices, Figure 13).
2. Applying the three channels Farun-Buddha, Firast and Zevs to the patient's head by imagining the patient's head as a bowl containing molten silver from which negative energy evaporates and leaves through the open patient's Lotus and uttering the names of the channels in any sequence until you intuitively feel that your work is complete. For example:
   "Farun-Buddha, Farun-Buddha, Farun-Buddha; Farun-Buddha-Firast, Farun-Buddha-Firast, Farun-Buddha-Firast, Firast, Firast, Firast; Zevs, Zevs, Zevs";

   again:

   "Farun-Buddha, Farun-Buddha, Farun-Buddha; Farun-Buddha-Firast, Farun-Buddha-Firast, Farun-Buddha-Firast, Firast, Firast, Firast; Zevs, Zevs, Zevs";

and again:

"Farun-Buddha, Farun-Buddha, Farun-Buddha; Farun-Buddha-Firast, Farun-Buddha-Firast, Farun-Buddha-Firast, Firast, Firast, Firast; Zevs, Zevs, Zevs" (until the practitioner feels their hands are warm)

at the end repeat many times "Zevs"

then repeat many times "Farun-Buddha-Firast, Farun-Buddha-Firast, Farun-Buddha-Firast, Firast, Firast, Firast";

finally repeat "Farun-Buddha" many times and remove hands.

The "cleansing the head" procedure should be conducted during each standard treatment session, for example, when working with such nervous and mental disorders as alcohol dependency, oligophrenia, cerebral spastic infantile paralysis, mental retardation, cerebral injury, and intracranial pressure. The procedure is also useful in improving the patient's intellectual and creative abilities.

Cleansing the Spine with the Golden Pyramid Channel

For cleansing the spine, you should approach the patient from the patient's back, put your hands on the patient's shoulders so that your fingers are in contact with the patient's spine. Both you and the patient stay within the golden ray, which emanates from the base of the Golden Pyramid and goes through the patient's head and spine down to the well. For full cleansing of the spine, you should then imagine a number of golden hemispheres appearing along the continuous flow of energy (golden ray) passing through the patient's spine. These hemispheres are picking up the "dirt" clustered along the patient's spine and pulling the "dirt" into the well. Termination of this image will close the Golden Pyramid channel.

6. Close the Well

To close the Well you need to imagine its lid much thicker and firmer than the initial lid you removed when you opened the Well. Imagine that the lid has sharp long spikes on its internal surface.

The Well for treatment sessions:

Visualize that some thick metal or concrete slab is shifted over the top of the Well that was opened for the whole room at the beginning of the session (paragraph 4). Check up the seal. If in your mind you can see some gaps between the walls of the room and the edges of the slab, you need to shift the slab backwards and then forward again until it seals the Well tightly.

The Well for "Motor-Well" method:

Visualize how you plug the Well up with a metal or concrete plug. Check up the seal. I there are some gaps you should unplug the Well and imagine the plug of the right size for the Well; then re-plug it the Well is sealed tightly.

7. Close the patient

Close the patient in reverse order as you opened them (see paragraph 3), i.e. close their feet, hands, abdomen, then back (if you opened it), chest, shoulders and the Lotus. The Lotus flower should be closed fully, but not tight.

If you had a few patients on the session you need to close them one by one, (i.e. close the patient's feet, hands, abdomen, chest, shoulders and the Lotus, then close second patient's feet hands, abdomen, chest, shoulders and the Lotus, and so on.)

8. Enlarge and align the patient's Aura

The patient's Aura can be expanded and aligned using the Farun-Buddha channel or a combination of the Farun-Buddha, Firast, and Zevs channels by:

- Placing your right hand over the patient's chest between the fourth and fifth Chakra while your left hand is placed parallel to your right hand from the patient's rear
- Setting an objective: "I would like to enlarge and align the patient's aura to the diamete of six feet (2 meters)" (see Appendices, Figures 14-16)
- Uttering the name of the Farun-Buddha channel or a combination of three channels in any sequence and imagining the patient's aura expanding to approximately six feet (2 meters in radius and smoothing out. If you have only the Farun-Buddha channel, you utter many times "Farun-Buddha, Farun-Buddha, Farun-Buddha, etc. If you have the Farun-Buddha Firast and Zevs channels, you utter:

"Farun-Buddha, Farun-Buddha, Farun-Buddha; Farun-Buddha-Firast, Farun-Buddha Firast, Farun-Buddha-Firast, Firast, Firast, Firast; Zevs, Zevs, Zevs";

again:

"Farun-Buddha, Farun-Buddha, Farun-Buddha; Farun-Buddha-Firast, Farun-Buddha Firast, Farun-Buddha-Firast, Firast, Firast, Firast; Zevs, Zevs, Zevs";

and again:

"Farun-Buddha, Farun-Buddha, Farun-Buddha; Farun-Buddha-Firast, Farun-Buddha Firast, Farun-Buddha-Firast, Firast, Firast, Firast; Zevs, Zevs, Zevs" (until the practitioner feels their hands are warm)

at the end repeat many times "Zevs"

then repeat many times "Farun-Buddha-Firast, Farun-Buddha-Firast, Farun-Buddha-Firast, Firast, Firast, Firast";

finally repeat "Farun-Buddha" many times and remove hands when the aura becomes six feet (2 meters) in diameter (like an inflatable balloon).

9.Thank the Channels

You should thank the Channels after each treatment session and every time you use them outside the sessions. When thanking the Channels you may address them the way you like (for example, "Thank you, Farun-Buddha channel, for your help")

Do not close the Channels! Ask your patients to open their eyes. The session is now finished.

Note: After the standard treatment session is over, the practitioner should always cleanse the premise where the session was held with the Firast channel.

SELF-TREATMENT

You can do treatment sessions on yourself by "contact" (touching) or "no-contact" (without touching) method.

Note: Self-treatment sessions must be conducted separately from the treatment sessions you do on your patients.

Procedure of the "contact" self-treatment session:

1) Stand straight, relax and close your eyes.

2) Open the channels on yourself.

3) Imagine that you are opening yourself beginning from the Lotus and down to your feet (in the same order as you do for your patients during treatment sessions).

   Imagine a phantom of your right hand. Then imagine a beam of bright light radiating from the forefinger of your phantom hand directed towards your body. Visualize how the beam makes opening cuts on your chest, abdomen, hands and feet (in the same way and order as you do when opening your patients during treatment sessions).

4) Open the Well.

5) Do healing work with your own chakras, internal body organs and clear your head using phantoms of your both hands. The "Motor-Well" method is to be done by phantoms of your arms and shoulders. Do not visualize a phantom of your full body. You only need to imagine phantoms of those parts of your arms and the shoulder that are actually used to pump the negative energy out of your body organs to the Well.

   You are NOT allowed to do any healing work for yourself using your real hands! You have to only use your phantom hands, arms and shoulders.

   You are NOT allowed to "write off" your own problems!

6) Close the Well.

7) Close yourself bottom-up.

8) Enlarge and align your own Aura (using phantoms of your hands)

9) Thank the channel(s) for help.

PASSWORD FOR OPENNING CHANNELS

1. Buddha, Buddha otkrivaju (open) kanal (channel) Farun-Buddha

(dlya ochischeniya, lescheniya, zaschiti) (for cleansing, healing and protection) Buddha

Farun – Buddha, Farun- Buddha, Farun – Buddha, Farun – Buddha, Farun- Buddha, Farun – Buddha...

Repeat n-times until you feel that the channel is opened

This opening password should be pronounced if you only have one channel Farunn- Buddha.

After you have been initiated into the Firast channel, you should use only one opening password for both channels Farun-Buddha and Firast:

2. Buddha, Buddha otkrivaju (open) kanal (channel) Firast (dlya ochischeniya, lecheniya, i zaschiti) (for cleansing, healing and protection) Buddha

Farun – Buddha --- Firast, Farun – Buddha --- Firast, Farun – Buddha --- Firast, Firast, Firast, Firast

Repeat 2-3 or n-times until you feel that both channels are opened

3. Otkrivaju (open) kanal (channel) Zevs:

Zevs, Zevs, Zevs, Zevs Zevs... - Repeat n-times until you feel that both channels are opened

4. Otkrivaju (open) kanal (channel) Anael:

Anaei, Anael, Anael, Anael, Anael, Anael, Anael, Anael... - Repeat n-times until you feel that both channels are opened

I. Buddha, Buddha otkrivaju (open) canal (channel) [name channel]

Buddha

Farun – Buddha --- [name channel], Farun – Buddha --- [name channel], Farun – Buddha --- [name channel]

[name channel], [name channel], [name channel]

Repeat 2-3 or n-times until you feel that both channels are opened

II. Otkrivaju (open) kanal (channel) [name channel]:

[Name channel], [name channel], [name channel] - Repeat n-times until you feel that both channels are opened.

EXERCISES

The exercises described below are aimed to help the practitioner activate their chakras, normalize their energy system, develop visualization skills (inner vision) and learn to achieve an "altered state of consciousness."

EXERCISE WITH A "CANNON-BALL"

Objective: to activate charkas and normalize work of energy system.

This exercise is aimed to activate the chakras and make them work in unison, i.e. direction and speed of all chakras' motion would be in synch.

Performing the exercise regularly for 3-5 min. every morning and evening will favorably affect your energy-system and will help you develop the ability to visualize things and processes.

Perform the exercise in the following order:

1. Stand straight (do always stand when doing this exercise) and imagine a cannon ball lying down on the floor behind you;

2. Imagine that your chakras are threaded on your spine and each chakra has a few wings (like a windmill);

3. Visualize that the cannon ball raises along the right side of your spine (see Appendices, Figure 17);

4. When the cannon ball raises along the spine it hits the chakras' wings and this makes the chakras to spin (like a windmill);

5. Two upper chakras (Ajna and Sahasrara) are not involved in the exercise;

6. Continue visualizing how after raising along the right side of your spine the canon ball moves over your head and then down along the left side of your spine. On the way down the canon ball touches the chakras' wings again that makes them spin faster.

7. Repeat this exercise with lifting and lowering the cannon ball a few times.

EXERCISE WITH A CANDLE

Objective: to achieve an "altered state of consciousness".

"Altered state of consciousness" is the condition of your mind when your consciousness "goes to sleep" or just "stops functioning" and, instead, your sub-consciousness starts working. In this condition your sub-consciousness will concentrate on receiving information from the candle's flame.

The exercise is to be done in the following order:

1. Prepare for the exercise by removing all external irritants (like TV, radio, phone, music-player, etc), mirrors and other reflectors;

2. Make sure no-one will disturb you while you are doing the exercise;

3. Take a thick candle and light it. Place the candle against some neutral background so that you would not see anything else but the candle's flame;

4. Switch all other sources of light off;

5. Place a candle at a comfortable distance (approximately 1,5m) from yourself. The flame should be approximately at eye level;

6. Choose some spot a little bit aside from the candle's flame and start looking at the spot (do NOT look at the candle's flame directly);

7. Your gaze should freeze on the selected spot. This is the main condition for being able to get the information out of your sub-consciousness (when working with the same information for a long time – in this case, it is concentration on the same spot - your consciousness will pause its activity and your sub-consciousness will switch on).

8. Keep staring at the same spot and thinking: "I would like to see the subtle body of the flame". Your strong desire will switch on certain programs of your sub-consciousness and your sub-consciousness will start providing you with the information about the energy-body of the candle. The longer your consciousness stops, the deeper you will be able to penetrate into the information.

9. Usual duration of the exercise is around 15-20 minutes. If you start feeling discomfort (physically or mentally) you should immediately stop doing the exercise.

EXERCISE WITH A PHOTOGRAPH

Objective: to achieve an "altered state of consciousness".

Exercise with a photograph is based on the same principle of stopping your consciousness's activity and receiving information out of your sub-consciousness as in the exercise with a candle.

You will need to have a photograph of a living person. It is better to use a passport photo or something similar as these kinds of photos are taken on a neutral background that does not carry any information so it will not interfere with the information about the person you are going to obtain. You cannot use photos of dead people or your own photo for doing the exercise.

1. Draw a dot in the top right corner of the photo. Place the photo on some support at the level of your eyes and at the distance comfortable for reading.

2. Keep staring at the dot wishing and aiming to see the energy-body of the person on the photograph. When your consciousness gets bored to process the same information (i.e. the dot) your sub-consciousness will switch on and will supply you with the information about the energy-body of the photographed person.

3. First you will see a thin glowing line around the contour of the person on the photo – it is the etheric body of the person. Then the next contour line that will appear around the person (this line will be wider, approx. 1.5 cm) – this is the astral body. The third glowing line (approx. 40 cm wide) will be the mental body of the person. If you keep staring at the dot you might see the next body, (i.e. karma body of the person in this case faces on the photograph will quickly change showing previous incarnations of the person.

ANATOMY CHART EXERCISE

Objective: to develop visualization skills (inner vision).

The best way to develop your visualization skills (inner vision) is to use an anatomy chart (see Appendices, Figure 20). It is recommended to work with your eyes open as this develops your inner vision better. When looking at the human's body organs in the book, do not concentrate your gaze at each organ, but try to view the whole body structure with a vacant look. With time you will be able to easily imagine all body organs separately, like the real ones.

When working with people, pathology in certain body organs can be identified as dark spots. For example, if you see a dark spot deeply in the chest area, it could mean that the patient is having problems with their lungs. If the dark spot appears to be on the surface of the chest, you can suggest breasts disease. If during or after a session, you notice new dark spots, leave them until the next session.

EXERCISES WITH DOWSING ROD

Objective: to develop visualization skills (inner vision).

Dowsing rod exercises are aimed to help the practitioner to further develop their visualization skills (inner vision).

The practitioner can work on the following dowsing rod exercises:

1. Exercise "Determining condition of the chakras and internal organs"

To determine condition of the chakras and internal organs, begin with the first Chakra using both the method of the dowsing rod and also your inner vision for better results. For this exercise, stand in front of the person and hold a dowsing rod at a 45-degree angle, regardless of whether you are right- or left-handed. Approach the person face to face and set a double intention: "I want to look at the first chakra and find out how it is working." Your sub consciousness will lead your inner gaze and direct it towards the first chakra. Reach agreement with your sub consciousness: If the first chakra is working well, your sub consciousness will tell you this by swinging the rod with maximum amplitude. The worse the chakra is, the smaller will the amplitude. Simultaneously, you will know the condition of the chakra using your inner vision. Previously you looked at the pictures of internal organs and chakras. The pictures of the first chakra (red circle) that you looked at before will be your reference, the standard. To find out if the chakra looks as the standard during the exercise, reach agreement with your sub consciousness: If the first chakra is balanced, your sub consciousness will show it, thus, there will be a red circle. The worse the chakra, the more deformations it will have (dirty-red circle, with dark spots, with deformities), and the rod will rotate. So the first method of determining the condition of the chakra coincides with the second.

Then work with the second, third, and all other chakras. When working with the seventh Chakra, hold the rod over the person's head. Reach agreement with your sub consciousness: if the seventh chakra is working well, your sub consciousness will show you this leading your hand and rotating with a speed, for example, one rotation per second. If the speed is smaller, this means that the person has a tendency towards depression. If the speed is more than 1 rotation per second, the person is aggressive.

Checking condition of the inner organs is performed next because each chakra is in charge of a certain part of the body. If, for example, the person's forth chakra is not working correctly, they have problems with their heart. If the third one is not working correctly, the person will have problems with organs in the abdomen (kidneys, liver, stomach, spleen, etc.). For example, your intention should be: "I want to look and find out the condition of liver." Your inner gaze is directed towards liver that should be imagined as a picture (with the same color, size, shape). If there are any problems with the liver, it will be imagined with some spots, outgrowth, of different color, thus, it will be different from the picture. In a similar way, determine condition of each organ and send a patient to perform full examination because you are not a doctor, therefore, you cannot determine a diagnosis. If the patient's internal organs are not in a bad condition and no drastic measures are necessary, heal the person yourself.

2. Exercise "Determining the "family curse"

Hold a dowsing rod in your hand with an objective to determine a "family curse": "I want to find out if this person has or does not have a "family curse" the way the person understands it. Everyone has their own understanding of the concept "family curse," and a specific person and their sub-consciousness knows themselves if they have a "family curse." If the dowsing rod does not turn, it means the sub-consciousness answers "No," and you can move on to the next question. If the rod turns, the answer is positive and in the patient's sub-consciousness there is full information on this subject, which through your relaxed consciousness will get to your head: Where did this curse come from? How did it happen? What these people looked like? What family side did the curse come from? You can ask this information from the dowsing rod or in other words, your sub-consciousness: Did it come from the mother's side? If the rod turns, ask the rod if the curse also came from the father's side. If the rod does not turn, then the curse is on the mother's side only. Then you can determine in which generation the curse happened. Arbitrarily, you can consider the parents to be the first generation, grandfathers and grandmothers – second generation, great grandfathers and great grandmothers – third generation, etc. While holding the dowsing rod, ask: "Is the curse from the first generation? And look at the result, etc.

3. Exercise "Determining deformations of the bio-field and the time when it happened"

Main type of deformations:

- Evil eye
- Curse
- Spell
- Break-up spells
- Encoding
- Brainwashing
- Influence with psychotropic weapon

To determine deformations of the bio-field, you will need to know the age of the person. If you have the person's picture, you can determine their age using the dowsing rods. When a person comes to your session, you can ask their name, age. You will use their age in this exercise. For example, if you are performing this exercise in a room, ask a person to stand from a wall so that there is space behind them. Mark the spot where the person is standing as their current age, and the spot where you are standing as the time of their birth. Make an "age scale", i.e. split the distance between the person and you into equal parts that correspond to their age. Perform this exercise in the same room and the person will be standing in the same room. This way, you can measure the distance precisely with a measuring tape and find the middle of the scale precisely. Set an intention: "I want to know when there were deformations of the person's bio-field." Reach agreement with your sub consciousness that it will direct your hand and move the dowsing rod when you get to the year the bio-field deformation occurred when you are going with the dowsing rod through the years on the age scale. For example, the dowsing rod approaches a year when there was a bio-field deformation, the rod moves and you mark this spot (place some object on that spot). Then continue going and marking the spots where the rod is moving until you reach the standing person. By the number of marks on the age scale, you will know how many deformations there were in the persons' life and at what age. Determine what happened during those years. What kinds of deformations are there? Curse, evil eye, spell, etc. Hold the rod and ask: "I want to know if there was the evil eye set on this person when they were 14 years old." If the rod does not turn, ask "Was there a curse?" If the rod turns, record an answer and ask what happened in the second deformation.

4. Exercise "Determining binding connections"

Binding connection is an energy-informational channel that goes from a specific chakra outwards through which the energy-informational flow goes. If the flow goes outward from the person, the person becomes a donor, and if the flow goes inward, such person is a "vampire." Binding connections are tied to chakras. The reasons for binding connections are emotions because when we express any emotion, the energy ejects, and the more the person expresses their emotions, the more energy they eject. Because of "necrotic connections" and other binding connections, a person can develop diabetes or asthma. That is why you should always keep yourself together. Not always does the lost energy get refilled quickly. It does not take a long time to get sick, but recovery always take time.

If the binding connection was formed in front of the patient's body, it is related to the future. If it was formed to the right, it is related to the present, behind – to the past, and to the left – it is a necrotic connection. For example, at work one person has feelings towards another, a man to a woman, or vice versa. He expresses feelings, so a channel (connection) in the front is formed because they live in separate places and see each other only at work. The connection is in the front because it is related to the future. The person who has feelings towards another will think about the future, make plans in their head to date, marry, etc. Time passes and plans become reality in the present; there are no plans for the future, but the feelings are still there, so the connection remains. It is not related to the future, but to the present, thus, it will be to the right of a person. After a while, the situation changes. The person towards whom the feelings were expressed leaves. He or she is gone, but the second person still has the feelings towards the person who left. The person is gone so there is no present connection between the people. The feelings are connected with the memories – with the past, and this connection will be from the back. Another situation. One of the people actually died, so the connection is to the left. The remaining person still has feelings that are expressed towards the deceased who is now in the other world. This connection is a necrotic connection of the first type (between a person and their deceased relative). If the necrotic connection of the first type is formed, in 80% of cases, a person will develop diabetes in a year, in 15% of cases – a bronchial asthma, in 5% - other illness. Diabetes could develop because of necrotic or other connections too, for example, connection to the home country. If a person left or emigrated from their home country, but they are still longing for their home, friends, close ones, this can cause diabetes. If a person with such illness came to you, you have to ask them when they got sick who in their family died when the person got sick. If there is a necrotic connection, it has to be removed from both sides – the living person and the deceased. To remove such connection, use the "writing off" method with a picture of a deceased person. "Write off" the connection from both sides – from the side of the living person and the deceased one because the connection could have been formed not only from the living to deceased, but also from the deceased to the living person. Do this every time the patient comes to a session until the illness is gone and they feel better.

There are three types of necrotic connections. The first one has already been described. The second type of necrotic connection is formed between a person and the other world when they are tricked into a contact with some "dark forces" of the spiritual world, but not because of their fault. The third type of necrotic connection can be formed by a person themselves when they connect to "dark forces" due to their ignorance. Many think that spiritual world is immaterial and does not cause harm, that it is only in the physical world that we should beware of the dangers and we can do whatever we want in the spiritual world. This is a big misconception. In the spiritual world, the negative forces can bring even more harm to a person if they do not know about this and intrude the spiritual world. For example, there are many books that talk about how to make yourself feel good. But making yourself feel good is ok if you received initiation into this knowledge. If you do something like this without initiation, it will cause harm because you do not have any protection. No spiritual practice can be performed if one has not received initiation into it. The same idea is true to Cosmoenergy. If you do not have initiations into channels, you cannot use them. If a person uses channels that they did not get initiated into, they will cause harm to themselves. If a person studies something without initiation, a necrotic connection is formed, which sometimes cannot be removed because the person needs to fully renounce.

For the binding connections exercise, imagine a person and their aura as an onion. If you take an onion and cut it, we will see a center of the onion. In this way, we can also imagine a person: physical body – the center of the onion, and around him/her the onion itself with layers – their aura. If there are some "necrotic" and other binding connections, they will stretch from the center of the onion through the layers. Binding connections and necrotic channels are energy-informational channels stretching from the chakras. Imagine a person with an intention: "I want to find out if there are any necrotic connections or other binding connections". Reach agreement with your sub consciousness that if the rod reaches the "necrotic connection" or other binding connection, your sub consciousness will move the rod by directing your hand where the flow goes. Hold the rod in your right hand at a 45-degree angle, regardless of whether you are right- or left-handed. Approach the person face to face and check on the left side of the person their necrotic connections. Set an intention: "I want to know if there is a necrotic connection." Mentally insert the rod between imaginary layers of the aura below the first chakra and move the rod to the left with an intention to find out if there is a necrotic connection. Reach agreement with the sub consciousness that if the rod approaches the necrotic channel, it will move. Depending on which direction the rod moves, you will know if the energy flow goes inward or outward. If you check with the rod and it does not move to the side, there are no necrotic connections. There is a rule: "Stand there where you have just checked." It means that if you have checked from the left, you will now have to stand at that spot and check from the back. Then stand in the back and check from the right. Then stand on the right side and check the front.

GENERAL RECOMMENDATIONS

1. Length of sessions and their frequency

The length of each session is 40 minutes. It is only if you are working with alcoholics, drug addicts or seriously ill people, you may conduct treatment sessions every day.

The treatment sessions should be conducted based on the following schedule:

1st week - three sessions per week
2nd, 3rd, 4th, 5th weeks - two sessions per week

The regular course of treatment is 10 - 15 sessions. After a full course of treatment, the patient goes on a "medical leave" lasting from three weeks to two months.

2. Working with the patient's photograph

When working with the patient's photograph, the standard treatment session is conducted as usual. It is allowed to work with chakras and body organs mentally.

3. Working with in-bed patients

When working with in-bed patients, either mentally or physically put your right (working) hand on a chakra in front (top) of the patient and imagine your left hand behind (underneath) the patient if you cannot actually put your left hand behind the bed-patient. Open the appropriate channels. Upon finishing the session, close the channels and the Lotus, and put your hands between the 4th and the 5th chakras and open a channel responsible for the main illness of the patient additionally (but not every bed-patient will need this additional treatment).

4. Charging water

Water, creams and other liquids can be cleansed by the Firast channel in a glass container by:

First Method:

- Opening the Firast channel and imagining light flow from the Firast channel emitted from the palm of their right hand over the glass container with water, cream, etc.
- Uttering the channel's name "Farun-Buddha, Firast; Farun-Buddha, Firast; Farun-Buddha, Firast; Firast, Firast, Firast" any number of times
- Keeping the flow of light from the channel Firast over the glass container until the practitioner intuitively feels like the liquid has been cleansed

- After the water has been cleansed with the Firast channel, it can then be charged by other healing channels that you need to use for healing the patients, for example, Saint Moses, Sinrakh, Sinlakh, etc.

Second method:

During the standard treatment session, the channels cleanse and charge water, creams, and other liquids automatically.

Note: It is recommended to use the second method of cleansing and charging water. The patient should drink the charged water before the next standard treatment session.

Though any water can be charged, some solutions (like water with sugar, or with salt) will charge the best; less - the usual water (spring water or filtered one); boiled water can only be charged a little; and distilled water does not charge at all as it is dead water. Charged water can be diluted. It does not have "shelf life" timeframe; more over, its charge will increase with time. It has been confirmed by joint research of Emil Bagirov and Dr. V. Sharkov. Using the same method as for charging water you can also charge cosmetics, bath salt, candles for clearing premises, etc.

Charged water is effective and multifunctional. It gives additional cleansing and healing effect; takes out salts, toxins and sand from our bodies; has laxative and diuretic effect; reduces appetite; increases healing effect for patients undergoing skin diseases treatment. Charged water can be used as a cosmetic remedy for rejuvenation or preventing loss of hair (it helps hair growth). Same water taken from the same source (tap) and charged by the same practitioner at the same session has different taste, smell and effect on different people.

Charged water must not be boiled or poured out (though, it can be heated). If you do not want to drink it, use the water for washing face or watering plants, but do not pour it out.

5. Working with channels

The most frequently used channels are Firast, Shaon, Farun-Buddha, and Zevs (they all can be opened at the same time). Other specialized channels that can treat the same illness (for example, the Risur and Saint Moses channels are both used for treating liver and stomach) should not be opened at the same time on the same patient. Simultaneous action of such specific channels will weaken healing effect. At first, choose one of the specific channels and use it during 4 or 5 sessions to treat the correspondent body organ. If no noticeable results were achieved during this time, start using the other specific channel that is also assigned for treatment of this body organ.

The more and longer the practitioner works with the channels, the more healing power they gain. The more treatment sessions conducted by their teacher or their senior colleagues the practitioner attends and the more they improve themselves, the cleaner their personal energy and healing skills will be.

6. Working with patients

If working with a new patient for the very first time, you should stay close near the patient for at least 2-3 minutes after opening channels on them. It is necessary because if there is a breach in the patient's chakra, the patient will fall down. To raise the patient, you will need to apply the Farun-Buddha channel between the 4th and the 5th chakras of the patient. If it is a child, do not let parents come close to the kid; and do not get scared of this situation. If the practitioner gets scared or worried, it will be more difficult for them to raise the patient. Why does it happen? It happens because when the Lotus or a channel gets opened, the patient can lose some of their "dirty energy."

Parents do not need to be present when you work with their children. You can also normally work with babies if their fontanel is not closed. Do not close channels on children because any excess energy will be emitted anyway.

When working with adopted children, you should also open (or initiate) a few channels on the foster mother, so the mother and the child always have positive energy around them.

A woman who went through treatments or who has been initiated into the channels will give birth to a gifted child. Childbirth process will go easy because the channels have restored her energy during her previous treatment sessions.

The channels do not close completely but reduce flow of energy through them so that the patient would not be overloaded with excess energy. Do not close channels at all when treating alcoholism.

7. Cleansing premises

Before and after each standard treatment session, the practitioner must cleanse the premises where the session will be/has been conducted using the Firast channel or other appropriate channels for cleansing premises (for example, the Glaikh Magister channel or the Deyen Zoroastrism channel). To cleanse premises, the practitioner should:

- Open the Firast channel and imagine a light flow from the Firast channel of dimension fitting the premises or object in question
- Utter the channel's name "Farun-Buddha, Firast; Farun-Buddha, Firast; Farun-Buddha, Firast; Firast, Firast, Firast" a number of times while imagining the light flow being emitted from the palm of their right hand
- Direct the flow of light from the Firast channel towards the object in question until the practitioner intuitively feels like the premise has been purified (This will increase the effectiveness of the purification session)
- Keep directing the flow of light until the practitioner intuitively feels that the object has been cleansed

8. Restrictions

Working with the following patients will require significant time commitment from a practitioner and can cause serious aggravations, which could be very difficult to handle by a patient and the practitioner. Lack of the practitioner's commitment and dedication will bring only insignificant results in curing the illness. However, if your close ones or relatives have these diseases, decide for yourself if you would like to work with them.

1. Patients with brain tumors
2. Pregnant women
3. Stage III and IV cancer patients
4. Patients with schizophrenia
5. Age restrictions (very old people)

9. Working with certain bodily organs:

1. The practitioner cannot place a drain and arcs on the following bodily organs:
    - Brain
    - The heart
    - Veins
    - Spine
    - Eyes

Note: In case of acute heart failure, call an ambulance. While waiting for a doctor, you can relieve the pain by using the "motor-well" method (pulling the "dirty energy," i.e. the pain in the heart chakra) without conducting a standard treatment session to prevent the patient from dying from pain shock.

2. It is necessary to place two arcs on each lung with a total of four arcs.

MORE ABOUT METHOD OF COSMOENERGY

The ancient knowledge of healing people, animals and plants by *channels of the Universe* is the greatest gift to Mankind that has been available to us from primordial time. The channels are made up of *constant, pure and invisible energy levels originating as a form of energy-information.* Thanks to modern-day research, the knowledge connected to healing by means of the channels has been revived. It is the knowledge that had long ago been discovered by the wise men of our past. For ease of reference, these Universal Channels have been named "**Cosmoenergy**".

A systematic method for the study and use of the channels for healing purposes has been and still is being unearthed and updated. It involves transmitting channels through the practitioner to the patient with attention and respect to the patient's various physical, mental or psychological illnesses, problems and difficulties. Thus, the approach and intended focus of the practitioner is on that of the whole person. The channels wash over and penetrate the physical and subtle bodies and consciousnesses of the patient while working towards gradual dissolvement of negativity on every level a given problem inhabits.

The method of Cosmoenergy does not work to heal separate areas of the human body, as does the clinically derived solution of a particular problem. Instead, the person is treated as a **single (whole) entity** rather than a set of bones, muscles and organs. Health and destiny do not exist separately from each other. During healing, the patient's destiny as well as their health changes for the better.

Channels are boundless and inexhaustible and possess cleaning, medicinal and protective properties. Harmony, love, creativity and beauty help us in reaching a clear, peaceful mind and consciousness, pure ideas and a sound body. Cosmoenergy practitioners are taught to help the people who come to them to improve for the best in all respects. *The purpose and goal of the Cosmoenergy practitioner* is not to merely ease the patient's condition for a span of time, *but to permanently get rid the patient of their illness*.

First and foremost of all, it is a hard work for the patient. The patients must work on themselves and strive to better their ills in every aspect of their thoughts, words and deeds. This self-censorship is an important part of healing, and it is what both patients, who wish to recover, and practitioners, who wish to heal, must strive for. As hard as it may be, we will always get help in these endeavors. The channels contain "programs" for healing our different bodies and states, from physical to emotional, for cleansing of objects and space surrounding us, and for protection from various negative influences. The channels are capable of penetrating the entire body, cleansing and supporting the well-being of each part of our body, each weakened cell. They aid in breaking up and dissolving negative deposits that have built up in us and fill us with vital strength and clarity.

The method of Cosmoenergy was initially intended for rendering assistance to a maximum number of people. The **channels will never cause harm to anybody or anything.** The uniqueness of this method consists of the practitioner's ability to direct the energy in order to influence every part of the patient's body; thus the practitioner is the conductor of pure cosmic "energy" who uses it for complex healing of the entire person. Up to today, more than one hundred active **healing channels** have been discovered and studied. The channels differ from each other by the nature of their properties.

The results of treatment by the method of Cosmoenergy are confirmed by studies in highly advanced medical clinics. The effect of channels' influence is obvious. **The list of cured illnesses shakes the imagination.** Cosmoenergy does not itself attempt to deny nor replace traditional medicine, homeopathy, acupuncture, etc.; it only supplements and expands them, proving in practice that the combination of ancient wisdom and achievements of our modern science results not in contradiction, but in an efficient and amazingly effective method of healing.

A person is a part of the Universe, part of the biosphere of Earth, and of their society. The human body is a system. All parts of the system (organs, for example) have information-energy components and, through them, the power of communication. If energy circulates correctly and the power balance is observed, bodies will never be ill. Normal circulation of energy in the person's body is influenced by many factors: weather conditions, the phases of the moon, the structure of the stars, the attitudes of surrounding people, character traits, the force of reaction to external events, etc. Everything in the Universe is interconnected; all of live and lifeless nature makes up a single organism, a single whole. This interrelation is manifested not only and not so much through direct physical contact of bodies with each other, but through the exchange of information-energy on the level of their energy fields. Mankind has always known the phenomenon of influencing people or objects from a distance. In the simple case of magnets, it is explained by the knowledge of magnetic energy fields around objects; in the case of an entire person, it is done through their bio-field.

The knowledge about existence of a human bio-field has its roots in great antiquity. It has long ago been scientifically proven that energy fields exist around the material bodies of all live and lifeless natural forms. A person's physical body consists of atoms and molecules that also possess fields. The combination of the individual fields on the atomic and molecular levels results in the entire bio-field of the person. One of the most important properties of a person's bio-field is that, according to the laws of physics and just as any other field, it is boundless. Modern devices are not capable of fully analyzing most of our bio-field because of its vast size and small relative intensity, but the bio-field directly around our physical body, the aura, is known to be registered by many modern devices. We now have diagnostics centers specifically designed for the study of auras as a combination of one's physical body and its bio-field.

Just as our physical bodies have their anatomy, our subtle bodies have theirs, which spatially correspond within the physical. The invisible energy centers, known as chakras, are really places of concentration of our subtle body energies. *The healthy functioning of chakras are essential in* Cosmoenergy, as the practitioner works to help these subtle energy centers maintain a level of maximum efficiency, purity and balance.

The first condition for those patients interested in beginning Cosmoenergy treatment sessions is gaining familiarity with the methodology of Cosmoenergy. The practitioner's work with a patient is measured in sessions and follows a certain procedure. First, the patient indicates which problems and symptoms are of their concern. Then the practitioner determines approximately how many sessions will be required to correct the imbalances and what assistance is necessary from the patient. The actual timing of the sessions is determined according to the patient and practitioner's schedules. The usual treatment frequency is 10-15 sessions, 1-2 months break. However, even during a break, the influence of the channels does not stop, so treatment is continual.

During the course of a session, which lasts about 40 minutes, the patient needs to stand in a comfortable, relaxed position with their eyes closed. The idea is to be relaxed enough to not resist or hinder the streams of directed energy that will be washing through and over you. If you feel like rocking back and forth, feel a desire to move your arms, back, a desire to bend down or even take a few steps, let you inclinations manifest themselves, even if they seem ridiculous. There are usually chairs placed behind you in case of any dizziness or fatigue to ensure that you feel safe and comfortable.

The recommended scheduling for the weekly healing sessions is 3 sessions in the course of the first week, 2 sessions in both the second and third weeks, and 1 or 2 sessions per week during weeks four, five and six. The time of each individual session is 40 minutes. Patients with difficult or deadly diseases, like cirrhosis of the liver, cancer, etc. have a different session schedule. These are special cases that are treated daily, even several times a day during the course of one to about three months. After that the frequency of the sessions decreases from several times a day to once a day, then once every 2 days, etc.

The method of Cosmoenergy promotes full harmonization of the entire human being, so it is inevitably a long therapy, ranging in time from a month and a half up to one year. Treatment of serious diseases for full recovery can last several years, but improvement of one's state of health and consequently one's destiny begins immediately after attending the first few sessions. During sessions, one's negative energy build-up, such as aggression, fear, hatred, anger, jealousy, etc., is purified. This alone promotes a more enlightened state of mind, possibility for spiritual growth, freedom from negative, impeding ideas, feelings, actions and people, inclinations towards narcotics and other intoxicating substances, suicidal thoughts, feeling of loneliness and despair. The actions of a person in the physical, visible world - their words, ideas, emotions, desires (kind or malicious) - neither disappear nor vanish completely. They remain within the space of subtle bodies invisible to us, our subtle energy. Therefore, the destiny and health of the person are influenced not only by their physical interactions with the world around them (words, actions). Emotions, desires and ideas expressed by us remain in space surrounding us. Bad ideas and unbridled emotions pollute this space: like attracts like! So, we once again reap what we have sown: love begets love, and anger begets anger. No immediate change on the physical plane occurs, yet changes on the subtle planes will not fail to pass. Projecting negative ideas in relation to another and suddenly receiving a much more vividly expressed negativity in relation to ourselves from an absolutely unexpected party, we often ask either ourselves or the unknown that we think has "punished" us the questions of "what for?" and "why?" Failures, problems, diseases, the presence of "bad luck", depression, chronic weariness, irritation, insomnia, loneliness, constant material problems and many other things are all manifestations of an overabundance of negative energy in ourselves! The channels are there to help us with these problems by removing the negative energies from where they built up in us, our chakra centers, and flushing them with pure, cosmic "energy". As a result, our diseases and problems disappear or come to pass in a less intense, easier way.

However, if the patient does not strive to keep the cleansed chakras in a purer state by filling their thoughts and emotions with love, positivity, joy, etc., they will not be able to get the full benefit of **Cosmoenergy**. **Cosmoenergy focuses on the harmonization of the entire person**; thus, it is designed to treat not just one disease or problem, but all. With serious diseases (such as chronic alcoholism, addiction, depression, epilepsy, etc.), treatment can last more than one year, all depending on the progress of the individual.

Thus, **it is a long therapy**, and improvements in a condition are replaced by the periods of worsened condition. This is normal and positive, and should be treated as a sign that the therapy is working. For full recovery from an illness, a great amount of negative energy must be removed, because in that lies the key to getting to the reason of the problem/illness, its root. All problems that the patient is experiencing must manifest themselves in a worsened state for a short period of time before leaving the patient forever. It is their way of exiting our subtle and physical bodies. This can happen through periods of various emotional states and worsened health. Aggravations can crop up even after it seems to you that you have completely recovered. It is very important to understand this aspect of the therapy, and to continue with treatment without anger and see it as an inevitable part of the recovery process. Whining, complaining, becoming angry or upset about this can only bring heavier, harder aggravations. If the patient strives to overcome their difficulties and works to improve their existing condition, the discomforts of the aggravations diminish quickly. But in any case, such periods are unavoidable for those wishing to recover. For this reason, before you set up times and begin going to sessions, it is necessary for you to determine whether you are ready to stand these "trials". Various unpleasant sensations, emotions and changes during and after the aggravated conditions are possible, as we mentioned above, but it is important to remember that all of them will gradually leave and calm down. Time and patience are necessary, and improvement in all affairs and conditions will come. But to receive this improvement joint work between you and practitioner is necessary. The work will not necessarily be very difficult, but it **is** necessary to achieve the desired change in oneself.

REMOVAL OF BINDING CONNECTIONS

We can create the binding energy connections with the deceased people ourselves when we do commemoration for the dead (not to be confused with "the service for the dead"). Every time when we do commemoration for the dead we, in a way, give the deceased permission to stick to us and suck our energy out.

The same permission we give to the deceased when we grieve for them, cry when we think about them, or speak badly about them. That is why it is said: "Say nothing but good of the dead". Do not make your life more complicated – do not disturb the dead.

In order to break a tied channel that drains your energy, you have to remove the energy binding connections with the deceased people you knew. To do this, you will need little church candles. The procedure can be performed in a church, temple, synagogue, etc. In the church, you begin with a prayer. If you do not know any prayers, simply talk to God in your own words. Then put candles in the place dedicated for candles for the peace of spirits. Light out a candle for the first dead person from your list and address the dead person by saying silently in your mind: "I am letting you go. Go to your world where you should be". Repeat the phrase 3 times. Do the same procedure for all other dead people you could recall and leave the candles at the church, temple, synagogue, etc. without touching them. You will need to light out one candle for each passed away person you could recall, say the same phrase to each of them. After you lit candles for all dead people you could recall, you can leave the church.

Perform this procedure 3 times, preferably in 3 different churches. Also, repeat the procedure every time when you see dead people in your night dreams.

HEALING CHANNELS OF THE BUDDHIST GROUP

Healing channels of the Buddhist group are included below. The "Yes/No" answers indicate whether or not the practitioner can charge water with the channel, apply the channel to aura and place an arc from the channel.

No.	NAME	APPLICATION	WATER	AURA	ARCS
1	FARUN-BUDDHA	Treatment of all ailments, including healing wounds and burns, normalization of blood circulation, stopping internal and external bleeding, treatment of gastric and duodenum ulcers, relieving entrapment of ophthalmic nerve, recovery from coma and fainting, relief of stress, shock, fatigue, dizziness and headache, treatment of gravely ill and elderly people. Purification of chakras, enlarging and aligning aura, providing protection and information.	YES	YES	YES
2	FIRAST	Treatment of most ear, nose, throat ailments, joint aches, nervous and mental disorders, enuresis, depression, stress, alcoholism, drug addition, insomnia, all benign and malignant tumors. Cleansing patient's head, neutralizing and removing evil eye, curses, malediction, etc. Cleansing water, creams, liquids, and premises. Purification of subtle bodies and restoring chakras' activity.	YES	YES	YES
3	KRAON	Treatment of all blood diseases, spleen, pancreas, liver, diabetes, hepatitis, anemia, leucosis, radiation sickness, immune system diseases, leukemia, intense bleeding, wounds, cuts, blood vessel ruptures, chronic hemorrhoid bleeding, ulcers, bleeding nose, severe menstrual bleeding, AIDS, alcoholism, drug addiction, depression. Normalization of blood constitution and endocrine system.	YES	YES	YES

No.	NAME	APPLICATION	WATER	AURA	ARCS
4	JILIUS	Treatment of all blood diseases, spleen, pancreas, liver, diabetes, hepatitis, anemia, leucosis, radiation sickness, immune system diseases, leukemia, intense bleeding, wounds, cuts, blood vessel ruptures, chronic hemorrhoid bleeding, ulcers, bleeding nose, severe menstrual bleeding, AIDS, alcoholism, drug addiction, depression, patients after chemotherapy. Normalization of blood constitution and endocrine system. High-powered channel.	YES	YES	YES
5	KURF	Straightening of children's scull bones (with open fontanel), removing intracranial and intraocular pressure, treatment of patients after hypertensive crisis	YES	NO	NO
6	SURIY-SANLAI	Treatment of all eye diseases, allergies, inflammations, nasopharynx diseases and severe allergic rhinitis, skin diseases, gangrene, vision correction.	YES	NO	YES
7	RANUL	Treatment of all eye diseases, including cataract and surgically treated eyes. High-powered channel.	YES	NO	NO
8	FARUN	Treatment of osteochondrosis, scoliosis, posture correction, polyarthritis (including infectious arthritis), and salt deposits.	YES	YES	YES
9	SAINT MUHAMMED	Treatment of allergies, wounds, severe and painful complications and inflammations after eye disease treatments; hormonal balance; removal of warts and fatty tumors, unwanted hair;	YES	NO	YES
10	SAINT JESUS	Treatment of upper respiratory infections, joints, fever; regulation of high and low blood pressure	YES	YES	YES
11	SAINT BUDDHA	Treatment of hernia, scars, fractures, injuries, joints, polyarthritis, salt deposits, pancreas, liver, gallbladder, spleen, prostate, gastrointestinal tract (stomach and intestine)	YES	NO	YES
12	SAINT MOSES	Respiratory tract, lungs, liver, adrenal glands, urinary system, gastrointestinal tract (stomach and intestine)	YES	NO	YES
13	RAUN	Treatment of alcoholism, drug addictions, relief of hangover and drug withdrawals, smoking cessation.	YES	YES	NO

No.	NAME	APPLICATION	WATER	AURA	ARCS
14	SINRAKH	Female rejuvenation, i.e. normalization of the hormonal system, smoothing out the wrinkles, tightening the skin.	YES	YES	NO
15	SINLAKH	Male rejuvenation, i.e. normalization of the hormonal system, smoothing out the wrinkles, tightening the skin, and erectile dysfunction treatment	YES	YES	NO
16	URAL	Treatment of cold (running nose, sore throat, bronchi), respiratory diseases, including viral respiratory infection, inflammation, meningitis, encephalitis and arachnoiditis.	YES	YES	YES
17	NINALIS	Treatment of flu, virus infections, allergies, heart and cardiovascular diseases, scars on the cardiac muscle (after a heart attack).	YES	NO	YES
18	SHAON	Removal of salt deposits, stones and sand from the body; treatment of nose neoplasms (adenoids and polyps) and sinusitis, migraine, lungs, respiratory track, nervous and mental disorders, all malignant and benign tumors, including myomas; improving cardiac function; purification of subtle bodies and removing negative influences; restoring chakras' activity.	YES	NO	YES
19	RISUR	Treatment of gastrointestinal tract (stomach, intestine, pancreas), liver, kidneys, spleen and adrenal glands, stomach cancer.	YES	NO	YES

HEALING CHANNELS OF THE MAGIC GROUP COMPATIBLE WITH HEALING CHANNELS OF THE BUDDHIST GROUP

Healing channels of the Magic group compatible with healing channels of the Buddhist group are included below. The "Yes/No" answers indicate whether or not the practitioner can charge water with the channel, apply the channel to aura and place an arc from the channel.

No.	NAME	APPLICATION	WATER	AURA	ARCS
20	ZEVS	Purification of chakras, cleansing patient's head, expanding and aligning aura.	NO	YES	NO
21	TATA	Normalization of hormonal balance and endocrine system; weight control and skin rejuvenation; thyroid treatment.	YES	YES	NO
22	TOR	Breaking down stones in the body; breaking down heavy clusters of dirty energy in the head.	NO	NO	NO
23	GOLDEN PYRAMID	Cleansing of the spine, healing of wounds and burns, cleansing of all types of witchcraft and brainwashing, protection of a patient and big areas (districts or countries) against diseases, natural disasters, Improvement of the ecological and social environment.	NO	NO	NO
24	LULIE	Treatment of schizophrenia (only for experienced practitioners), mental and nervous disorders, Cerebral Spastic Infantile Paralysis (CSIP), weight gain/loss.	NO	NO	NO
25	GEKATTA	Breast enlargement and breast shape correction, treating all breast and gynecological diseases, excluding mastitis and tumors	NO	NO	YES
26	TITAN	Only for activating chakras (in severe cases when chakras are not activated using the channels Zevs + Firast + Farun-Buddha)	NO	NO	NO

No.	NAME	APPLICATION	WATER	AURA	ARCS
27	BONN	Facilitation of seriously ill, bed-patients, post-traumatic patients, stroke patients; developing levitation abilities.	NO	NO	NO
28	SOUTRA-KARMA	Partial or full removal of karmas (up to 7th generation).	NO	NO	NO
29	MOONLIGHT CHANNEL	Relieving any pain, for example, toothache, wounds, and cuts.	NO	NO	NO
30	HUTTA	Treatment of all diseases in very complex cases and when recovery of the disease is delayed.	NO	NO	NO
31	AGNI-KHUM	Treatment of all illnesses, especially severe illnesses.	NO	NO	NO

CHANNELS OF THE MAGIC GROUP INCOMPATIBLE WITH HEALING CHANNELS OF THE BUDDHIST GROUP

Channels of the Magic group incompatible with healing channels of the Buddhist group are included below. The "Yes/No" answers indicate whether or not the practitioner can charge water with the channel, apply the channel to aura and place an arc from the channel.

No.	NAME	APPLICATION	WATER	AURA	ARCS
32	MAMA	Calming and stress relieve, purification of gravely sick patients, nourishment and rehabilitation, treatment of insomnia, removal of binding connections to the lower (negative) world, removal of an evil curse, the evil eye, witchcraft and return it to the originator if the patient believes he/she was under such impact	NO	NO	NO
33	MIDI	Providing information on patient's problems and suitable healing methods; assisting in locating, bringing home lost people and arranging meetings between people; increasing sensitivity when working with bio-location frames and/or dowsing; protecting against negative forces (only if used by a Master).	NO	NO	NO
34	GEKTAS	Providing information on patient's problems and suitable healing methods; increasing sensitivity when working with bio-location frames and/or dowsing; protecting against negative forces).	NO	NO	NO
35	ANAEL	Creating a favorable and friendly attitude towards a person and those influenced by the channel's energy, evoking within a person such qualities as mercy, compassion and unconditional love, preventing and ending arguments, fights and disputes, changing the emotional state of a person transforming that person's state of mind into a kind and happy one.	NO	NO	NO
36	FIRST MAGIC CHANNEL	Cleansing, protection, removal of curses, spells, shocks, malediction, etc.	NO	NO	NO

No.	NAME	APPLICATION	WATER	AURA	ARCS
37	SANCTIFICA TION OF OBJECTS CHANNEL	Removing the dirty energy and purifying/sanctifying food, cloths, water, jewelry, gold, goods, cars, mechanical objects, machines, etc. with the clean, light energy.	NO	NO	NO
38	LUGRA	Treatment of all diseases of any animals, birds, fish, reptiles, insects, plants, etc.	NO	NO	NO
39	AGNI	Rejuvenating, energizing, cleansing, and improving vitality of a patient; removing stress and depression.	NO	NO	NO
40	KHUM	Purifying and calming down a patient; eliminating depression, stress, aggression; suppressing fights, quarrels, drunken brawls, riots	NO	NO	NO
41	DO	Astral travel	NO	NO	NO
42	RATKHA	Protecting the practitioner in case of a threat to their life	NO	NO	NO

BIBLIOGRAPHY

1. Bagirov, Emil. <u>Cosmoenergy Textbook</u> Moscow: Zolotoi Telyonok, 2009.
2. Bagirov, Emil. <u>Handbook of Cosmoenergy Practitioner</u> Moscow: Zolotoi Telyonok, 2013.
3. Fusu, Larisa and Emil Bagirov. <u>Healing Cosmoenergy</u> Moscow: Zolotoi Telyonok, 2005.
4. Fusu, Larisa and Emil Bagirov. <u>Practical Work with Cosmoenergy Channels</u> Moscow: Library of Classic Cosmoenergy School by Emil Bagirov, 2005.
5. Sharkov, V.F. and Emil Bagirov. <u>Material projections of "subtle energy."</u> <u>Experiments with water and water solutions</u> Troitsk: Torvant Press, 2004.

APPENDICES

ILLUSTRATIONS

Figure 1 "The Shell"

Figure 2 "Golden Pyramid"

Figure 3 "Open the Channels"

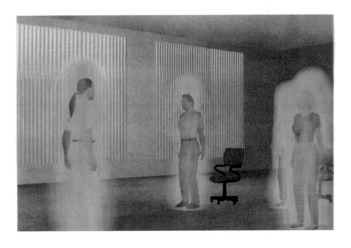

Figure 4 "Open the patients"

Figure 5 "Writing off problems"

Figure 6 "Working with the Second Chakra"

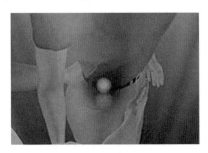

Figure 7 "Working with the Fifth Chakra"

Figure 8 "Working with the Fourth Chakra"

Figure 9 "Method "Motor-Well"

Figure 10 "Work with problems" Step 1

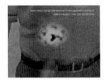

Figure 11 "Work with problems" Step 2

Figure 12 "Work with problems" Step 3

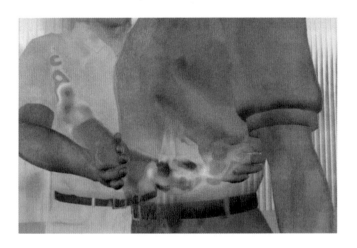

Figure 13 "Cleansing the head"

Figure 14 "Enlarging and aligning the aura"

Figure 15 "Enlarging and aligning the aura"

Figure 16 "Enlarging and aligning the aura"

Figure 17 "Exercise with a "cannon-ball"

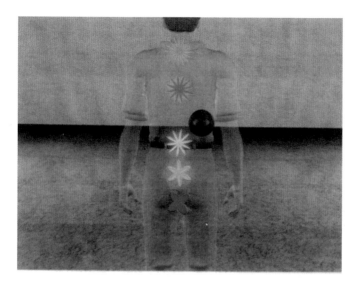

Figure 18 Spinal Cord and Skull of a Person and Chakras

Spinal Cord and Skull of a Person
and Chakras

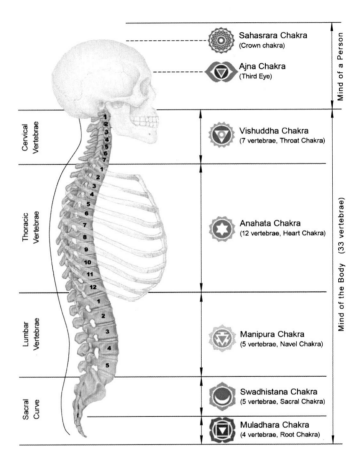

Figure 19 Chakras and Bodily Organs

Chakras and Bodily Organs

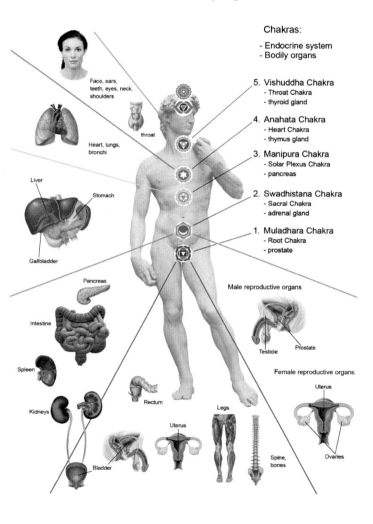

Chakras:
- Endocrine system
- Bodily organs

5. Vishuddha Chakra
   - Throat Chakra
   - thyroid gland

4. Anahata Chakra
   - Heart Chakra
   - thymus gland

3. Manipura Chakra
   - Solar Plexus Chakra
   - pancreas

2. Swadhistana Chakra
   - Sacral Chakra
   - adrenal gland

1. Muladhara Chakra
   - Root Chakra
   - prostate

Face, ears, teeth, eyes, neck, shoulders

throat

Heart, lungs, bronchi

Liver

Stomach

Gallbladder

Pancreas

Male reproductive organs

Intestine

Spleen

Testicle   Prostate

Kidneys

Female reproductive organs

Rectum

Uterus

Legs   Uterus

Ovaries

Bladder

Spine, bones

Figure 20 Human Anatomy

Human Anatomy

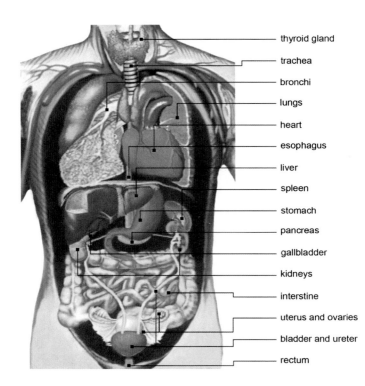

- thyroid gland
- trachea
- bronchi
- lungs
- heart
- esophagus
- liver
- spleen
- stomach
- pancreas
- gallbladder
- kidneys
- interstine
- uterus and ovaries
- bladder and ureter
- rectum

APPLICATION FORM

Applicant's Full name:_____

Date of birth: _____

Home/Postal Address_____

_____

Phone: _____

E-mail: _____

Date: _____

To the attention of:

Letter of Application

I would like to complete the course in the period from «___»_____20__ to «___»_____20__. I herewith acknowledge that I am familiar with and accept the terms and conditions of the course.

_____   _____

Applicant's full name   **Applicant's signature**

2 photos (color) of the Applicant are attached.

Where did you learn about the course from?

_____

REGISTRATION CARD

Passport size
photo

Last name: _____

First name: _____

Date of birth: _____

Sex: Male / Female

Home address: _____

Education: _____

Current workplace: _____

Position: _____

Initiation into Channels: _____

_____

_____

Teacher: _____

DISCLAIMER

I have received the full information concerning the method of Cosmoenergy. I understand that this method will provide me only with benefits, help me relieve stress, lead to a more balanced state of mind, and revert the negative changes in my body that led to my diseases/problems.

I know that this method is conductive to the full harmonization of my body.

I know that this method does not deny nor replace modern medicine; it is not used to diagnose, prescribe, cancel or change the dosage of the taken medications that were prescribed to me by my attending doctor.

I am informed that I should begin to notice all positive changes occurring in my every day life and share them with the practitioner beginning from the first treatment session to provide the practitioner with feedback and dialogue to enhance my treatment.

I am informed about possible aggravations and various feelings/sensations during and after the course of treatment.

I know that if during the treatment sessions I do not feel anything, it does not mean that the method is not working.

I am informed that the treatment consists of more than one treatment course and that I should follow a specific schedule of treatment sessions with the break between the treatment courses.

I know about the necessity of my self-development and work on my flaws and imperfections with which I came to the practitioner and that I have to make every effort to live in such a way that my thoughts, words and deeds are in harmony, that I should strive not to stress, shout, swear, think and act negatively towards other people, that I have to cope with my negative thoughts, laziness, anxiety, inactivity, etc.

Signature_____

Full Name_____

Date_____

Telephone_____

Address_____

Do you use any other methods of treatment?_____

Who referred you or how did you learn about this method?_____

Made in the USA
Las Vegas, NV
01 June 2024

90603086R00057